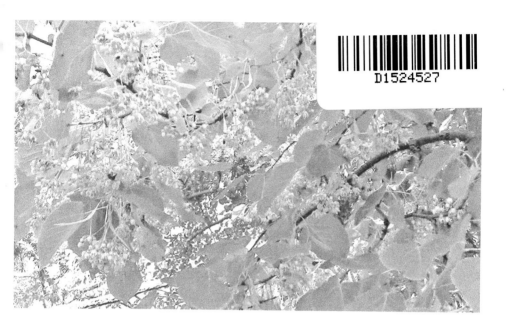

Flower Power

Establishing Pollinator Habitat

Tammy Horn Potter

ISBN 1-878075-56-X

978-1-878075-56-7

www.wicwas.com

Page 1 photo:
Basswood tree in bloom. Picture taken by Will Overbeck. June 18, 2013.

Cover photos:
Mike Connor (tulip poplar, UR), USDA (sunflowers, UL).
Bo Sterk (bees emerging, LM)
All others by the author.

Back cover:
Author's photo Joseph Rey.

Photo code:
U = Upper
L = Lower
M = Middle
UL, UR = Upper Left, Upper Right

In 1997, after completing a Ph.D., in literature, Tammy Horn Potter volunteered to help her grandfather with his beehives for one day. Twenty years later, Horn Potter is still keeping bees on that same farm. She wrote *Bees in America: How the Honey Bee Shaped a Nation* (UP of KY, 2005) and *Beeconomy: What Women and Bees can Teach Us about Local Trade and the Global Market* (UP of KY, 2012). In 2006-2010, she worked during winter seasons for Big Island Queens. In 2008, she started Coal Country Beeworks, working with surface mine companies to establish pollinator habitat and apiaries in Eastern Kentucky. In 2014, she became the Kentucky State Apiarist, coordinating the Kentucky Department of Agriculture Pollinator Protection Plan. From 2015-2019, she has coordinated the USDA Honey Bee Health Survey in Kentucky. She also serves on the boards of Eastern Apiculture Society, Project Apis M, Foundation for the Preservation of Honey Bees, Green Forests Work, and Kentucky State Beekeepers Association.

Author Picture by C. Bishop, 2013.

The Greeks had a word, *xenia*—guest friendship—a command to take care of traveling strangers, to open your door to whoever is out there, because anyone passing by, far from home, might be God. Ovid tells the story of two immortals who came to Earth in disguise to cleanse the sickened world. No one would let them in but one old couple, Baucis and Philemon. And their reward for opening their door to strangers was to live on after death as trees— an oak and a linden—huge and gracious and intertwined. What we care for, we will grow to resemble. And what we resemble will hold us, when we are us no longer....

The Overstory, Richard Powers

Acknowledgments

To the following people for assistance with Coal Country Beeworks: Ed and Elaine Holcombe, Dr. Alice Jones, Allen Meyers, Paul Rothman, Dr. Don Graves, Dr. Patrick Angel, Don Gibson, John Tate, Brian Patton, Bob Zik, Stacey Billiter, Robert Ray, David and Susie Duff, Dr. Chris Barton, Charles May, Jacob Stewart, Alice Whitaker, Krista Whitaker, Mary Sheldon, Michael French, Stanley Glowacki, Jerry Hayes, Green Forests Work, the Steele-Reese Foundation, Kentucky Foundation for Women, Foundation for the Preservation of Honey Bees, and the Kentucky Agriculture Development Board.

To the following people for assistance with the Kentucky Department of Agriculture Pollinator Protection Plan: Commissioners of Agriculture James Comer and Dr. Ryan Quarles, Keith Rogers, Dr. Robert Stout, Columbia Gas Vegetation Management Team members Susan Murray, Tony Tipton, Stan Vera-Art, Colby Tisdale, Robert Hoffman, John Pitcock, Michaela Rogers, John Seymour, Lewis Bradley, Dr. Ric Bessin, Michaela Rogers, Ellen Mullins, Mike Smith, David Cornett, Dr. Jen O'Keefe, and Dr. Deb Davis

In Chapter Three I have included, where possible, species in which pollen grains were found in honey samples analyzed by Dr. Jen O'Keefe at Morehead State University or Dr. Vaughn Bryant at Texas A&M. Both O'Keefe and Bryant specialize in a skill known as melissopalynolgy, i.e., the identification of pollen grains found in honey.

And to Dr. Dick Scott, for his tenacity; photographers Kit Cottrell, Michael French, Lyn Hacker, Mike Connor, K. Black, C. Bishop, S. Brundage, J. Marcus, C. Radcliffe, Joseph Rey, Bo Sterk, S. Glowacki, T.C. Davis, L. Steidel, Larry Connor, USDA, W. Overbeck, Janine Perry, K. Sharma, S. Buckley, M. Sharp, Dr. Jen O'Keefe and Dr. Vaughn Bryant; Charlene and Earl Horn, Eugenia and John Potter; my editor, Larry Connor, and my husband Douglass Woods Potter.

All photos by the author unless otherwise indicated.

TABLE OF CONTENTS

PREFACE

People ask me how I transitioned from an English professor to a state apiarist. It is a fair question because in college, I was determined never to pursue a career in math, science, or agriculture. After growing up with farm chores in all types of unpredictable weather, I equated a college education to an escape from the farm's relentless schedule. I lived in a 100+ year-old farmhouse, so I wanted "temperature control" instead of the seasonal demands of taking care of animals and plants, especially in the cold winters. I set my mind to become an English professor, which I thought would guarantee relative comfort near a thermostat.

T.R. Hacker, who grew up in Leslie County, KY. Hacker is harvesting honey in his apiary located in Fayette County. L. Hacker. 1997.

In 1997, after defending my dissertation, I came home to Kentucky for a brief vacation and offered to assist my grandfather T.R. Hacker with his honey bees. I was just relaxing after a "down to the wire" finish of the dissertation.

The first moment we opened a hive in early May, I inhaled the buttery scent of beeswax mixed with fermenting pollen and have remained intoxicated. I write this, not because I am proud that I avoided sciences so long, but because my dog-legged career from the humanities to applied sciences may give someone else courage to step outside a comfort zone, one's "mind-forged manacles" as the English poet William Blake would say. Since 1997, I have immersed myself in apiculture, "farming for intellectuals," according to Sue Hubbell in her work, *A Book About Bees: And How to Keep Them*. Because the honey bee hive makes sense to me when so many other realms do not, I use it as a point of reference to guide me to learn more about its caste system, to its floral sources, to the queen bee production industries, to opportunities to create more pollinator habitat acre by acre, foot by square foot. Now, I do math, science, and agriculture on a daily basis—and I love it.[1]

[1] Sue Hubbell, *A Book About Bees: And How to Keep Them*, New York: Houghton Mifflin, 1988. 53.

INTRODUCTION

A football field is one and a third acres, including the end zones. This image is useful when considering large land projects such as surface mine sites, utility rights-of-ways, landfills, and other extractive industries. Some surface mine sites are 3,000 acres and have been operating for twenty to thirty years with the transitions in reclamation technology and policy clearly visible as you drive across the site. Other surface mine sites are smaller and active with blasts happening a mile away. Because many people no longer live on farms, I fear the word "acre" may have lost any frame of reference. However, I will be using this term repeatedly, so it is handy to have a common point of reference. A football field is a good transition between agriculture and sports.

In 2006, I was serving as the National Endowment of Humanities Chair of Appalachian Studies at a private liberal arts college when I first looked over a surface mine site that was 2,000 acres. My first book, *Bees in America: How the Honey Bee Shaped a Nation*, had just been released. I was beginning my second book when I decided to take a brief break to trek to a mountain top

Aerial view of a surface mine site, K. Cottrell, 2006.

Sericea lespedeza. The Missouri Department of Conservation offers many tips for controlling this invasive ground cover: https://mdc.mo.gov/trees-plants/problem-plant-control/invasive-plants/sericea-lespedeza-control

removal site in Perry County, Kentucky.[2] I made this trip along with artists, authors, and environmentalists invited by Kentuckians for the Commonwealth, an environmental group. Our objective was to survey reclamation practices on surface mine sites in Eastern Kentucky.

At the beginning of early summer, the Appalachian Mountains in Eastern Kentucky are a dense, diverse undulating forest spread over fifty-four counties with sinewy rivers and power lines snaking their ways around clearings for towns and houses. Spring in Kentucky is remarkable for its lush forest canopy.

Yet, our group saw massive fragmented areas in the forest canopy, several thousand acres in size, most of which covered not by trees but by an invasive ground cover called *Sericea lespedeza*. The specific site that Kentuckians for the Commonwealth visited in 2006 is called a "legacy site," a former coal mine site that had been released from federal oversight but still owned by a coal company.

Because chief concerns of a surface mine company (or any extractive industry) are controlling potential floods and erosion, the site had been monitored by the federal reclamation policies defined by the 1978 Surface Mining Control and Reclamation Act (hereafter referred to as SMCRA). The soil had been compacted, making it too difficult for many trees to establish extensive root systems. The only plants thriving were invasive ground covers and/or introduced shrubs such as autumn olive (*Elaeagnus umbellata*). At the time, I did not appreciate the complexities represented by autumn olive. Introduced in 1830s to the United States as an ornamental, autumn olive grows quickly and creates a shade barrier, displacing other species that need sun. As invasive

---

[2]Surface mine sites became regulated by the Office of Surface Mining in 1977 with the Surface Mining Control and Reclamation Act.

U: Mature autumn olive (*Elaeagnus umbellata*). Perry County. 2012. Dense width creates shade, displacing other species. LL: Autumn olive bloom produces pollen in the early spring and a light nectar that makes very light honey. Beekeepers and pollinators appreciate this plant as an early source of nutrition. LR: Birds devour these berries in the fall. LL: Autumn olive can bloom as early as March or as late as mid-April in the Appalachians.

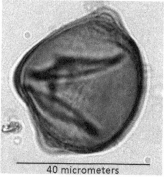

40 micrometers

L: Autumn olive (*Elaeagnus umbellata*) pollen, polar view. J. O'Keefe.
R: Autumn olive (*Elaeagnus umbellata*) pollen, equatorial view. J. O'Keefe.

as it is, honey bees benefit from its nectar and pollen, with many beekeepers making a honey crop from this one species. The honey bees can build up on the pollen, and by the time other species such as black locust and tulip poplar bloom, the hives are at the population needed to take advantage of those nectar flows (40,000 honey bees in one colony is ideal for honey production). In the fall, birds appreciate its red berries and scatter seeds across the disturbed mine site areas via defecation. The complexities of autumn olive force me to acknowledge that reclamation is not linear. With every adjustment made to an approved plant list, there are winners and losers. At a time when the United States loses on average one in every three hives, I find that the autumn olive is beneficial to honey bees in Appalachia. However, I am certainly not an advocate of this plant, and it is no longer an approved species to plant for reclamation plans.

Even though a key component of the SMCRA legislation is that reclamation should plant species that had existed prior to mining, the soil compaction resulted in the lack of diversity of plants. In lieu of being able to get native hardwoods to grow successfully, civil engineers had adopted an approach to simply, "make sites green again," explained Dr. Don Graves, inadvertently creating a pastoral landscape instead of a mesophytic forest.

Standing on that ridge, staring at that *Sericea lespedeza*, I decided to collect environmental impact statements (hereafter referred to EIS) of surface mining impacts on pollinator habitat. My plan had been to collect these EIS statements from 2006-2007 and compile a best management practices plan that could be used to include pollinator habitat in reclamation practices. Appalachian surface mines account for approximately 2,272 acres of deforested land, although that number has been declining as coal has declined in electricity production. Yet, in February 2007, I had *zero* environmental impact statements to show for my research. After making numerous phone calls, I was incredulous that environmental impact statements may not exist for pollinator habitat. Environmental impact statements exist for snail darters. They

"Pastoral look" is a result of the compaction of surface mine sites, a "legacy" site in this book. Hives were placed at this site in 2010, and students have planted trees and sown wildflowers as well. 2010.

exist for salamanders. They exist for running buffalo clover and other flowering species. Yet pollinators, which contribute approximately $21 billion to the agricultural food economy, have no such federal oversight. I kept calling around various state and federal bureaucratic entities, loving nothing more than being on a quixotic mission on behalf of pollinators.

During one phone call with the Kentucky Division of Natural Resources, an exasperated office assistant told me to call Paul Rothman, who was in charge of the division. At that time, Rothman answered directly to the Governor of Kentucky. "Paul Rothman is a tree guy," the assistant explained. "He loves trees as much as you love honey bees. If anyone in the state would know the numbers of trees, it would be he."

So, I called Paul Rothman and asked, quite bluntly, "How many bee trees are being cut down on surface mine sites"?

What followed was a very long pause. I was unprepared for the polite response when it finally came.

"Ma'am, I don't know what a bee tree is, but if you tell me, I will help you plant them."

I accepted Rothman's invitation to visit Starfire Mine Site, a surface mine site in which soil compaction was reduced. Along with Dr. Don Graves (University of Kentucky Forestry), the three of us traipsed through the University of Kentucky experimental tree reforestation plots and could see improvements to forestry if a reduction in compaction and modification to topsoil could be put in place prior to planting trees.

L: Dr. Don Graves (ret. University of Kentucky Forestry professor), R: Paul Rothman, director of Kentucky Department of Natural Resources Cabinet (ret.). At the Starfire reforestation research plots, Perry County. 2007.

Don Gibson, Reclamation Officer. C. Bishop, 2008.

By August 2007, I was no longer the NEH Chair of Appalachian Studies. I was unemployed. However, as a result of meeting with Rothman and Graves at Starfire Surface Mine Site, I had work to do. Rothman, Graves, and I discussed plant species, bloom times, nectar production, pollen availability, and other opportunities. These meetings led to conversations with coal companies, specifically Don Gibson, to discuss a strategy for developing forest-based apiculture. Is it feasible to obtain funds to create pollinator habitat on surface mine sites? Where could those funds be obtained? Could there be such an entity as an "extension-research-reclamation apiary program" at a state university?

At the time, there were no templates for such a venture, but it seemed worth trying to define one. Eastern Kentucky University had just opened its Eastern Kentucky Environmental Research Institute. Its director, Dr. Alice Jones, had been successful in obtaining a National Science Foundation grant to pursue collaborative alliances among diverse stakeholders, resulting in improved science that would benefit—and most importantly—stay in the region. The National Science Foundation had observed that many scientists "cut their teeth" in the Appalachians, do promising research, but then leave the region, taking their expertise with them. The Eastern Kentucky Environmental Research Institute was designed, in theory, to provide a framework for not just science to be done, but to create a community in which science could be supported in the long run. It could accept funds from a variety of sources to support science in the region.

As it so happens, a Tennessee queen bee producer named Edwin Holcombe and his wife Elaine had long-wanted to support such an entity. Ed had traveled to Azerbaijan and Armenia to help beekeepers learn queen production skills and honey production techniques. "I would love to do something similar in the United States," he once remarked for an article I wrote about his beekeeping travels in 2005. I worked with Dr. Jones to create a one-year budget that I submitted to Edwin and Elaine and their accountant in 2007.

Most universities have foundations by which a benefactor can give a gift, in this case to the Eastern Kentucky Environmental Research Institute, but projects must also benefit students. The Holcombes provided a gift for one year, and we created Coal Country Beeworks to increase pollinator habitat, provide education and extension, and do research. While there were no guarantees that other grants would be funded, the possibility of being able to establish apiaries on mine sites was so promising that it seemed foolish not to try.

As difficult as the process of getting Coal Country Beeworks launched in 2008, I thought then, and still do now, that I would have had enormous regrets if I let this opportunity pass by because of my pride. There are tangible results, of course: an annual beekeeping school meets every January, work with other nonprofits to plant tree seedlings continues apace, and even though the East-

Ed and Elaine Holcombe and Eastern Kentucky Environmental Research Institute team, Dr. Alice Jones, Krista Whitaker, Karrie Adkins, Hannah Watts, Tammy Horn Potter, 2007. C. Radcliffe.

ern Kentucky Environmental Research Institute no longer functions at Eastern Kentucky University, the friendships have led to many opportunities reflective of the National Science Foundation vision. The Environmental Research Institute was hardly a waste of taxpayer money.

As I write this book, I serve as the Kentucky State Apiarist, hired in 2014 by the Kentucky Department of Agriculture. As part of the Kentucky Department of Agriculture Pollinator Protection Plan, I collaborate with multiple stakeholders to coordinate efforts to minimize costs while increasing pollinator habitat on various rights-of-ways that they control. Most of these efforts simply extend the efforts led by Coal Country Beeworks. The lessons can be extended to other industries and non-profits—and perhaps with less challenges.

The Scandinavians say their forests "are the mantle for the poor."[3] Forests provide the following for civilization: wood for shelter, furniture, warmth, and tools; fruits, nuts and acorns for food for humans and livestock; and nectar and pollen for syrups and honeys. Even as civilization has become more industrialized, timber fueled those expansions. Because humans take forests for granted, we lose sight of their importance. In the United States, I see the potential for a forest-based beekeeping initiative that would set up five different lines of beekeeping income: honey production, wax production, queen bee production, pollination contracts, and knowledge-based careers such as extension or research. Both trees and beekeepers require a long "turnaround" time before they are productive. Most trees do not generate a return for their investment until they are at least five-ten years old. Similarly, in the beekeeping world, one will be a beginner for ten years, about the same time a tree will mature.

Although the U.S. has become accustomed to importing honey from Asia and beeswax from Africa for cosmetics, the Appalachian region is a "sleeping giant" for forest-based beekeeping. As the region transitions from a fossil-fuel based economy, beekeeping-based reforestation can be part of the new economy, and more generally, the increase of pollinator habitat across the nation. In 2008, with the invaluable assistance of my colleagues, we launched Coal Country Beeworks, and its mission was simple: A diverse economy depends upon a diverse landscape. The challenges were, and continue to be, immense. Estimates are that the planet will eventually be home to twelve billion people. The Appalachian region is in the throes of a massive drug epidemic that threatens to defray the generational fabric that has held the region together despite a century of negative stereotypes, lackluster political policies and "colonialization" that tends to appropriate resources away from education and funnels them toward other efforts outside the region. The benefits are that vast acreages are not contaminated by industrial agricultural

[3]Michael Williams, *Deforesting the Earth, From Prehistory to Global Crisis*. Chicago: U of Chicago Press, 2002, p. 90.

Professional tree planters from Williams Forestry and Associates, Pike County Kentucky, planting on ripped mined land. The prescription was an upland oak/shortleaf pine mix, with wildlife shrubs for pollinators, fruits. Green Forests Work 2015. M. French.

and suburban pesticides and the diversity of native trees produce unique floral honeys unmatched anywhere else in the world in a nation persistently short of honey. With unemployment stubbornly high even as the rest of the nation recovers from the Great Recession of 2008, Eastern Kentucky can take advantage of these factors to supplement its economy and enrich livelihoods with its own "flower power," forming and relying on its "mantle for the poor."

CHAPTER ONE: HONEY BEES

Numbered Purdue queen bee. Most queens cost about $25-50.00, but this queen is a breeder queen and costs about $250.00. Her workers will defend themselves from a parasite called a varroa mite. This behavior trait is genetic and heritable. 2017.

For many people, an immediate image of a honey bee hive is one in the middle of summer, with many bees in frenetic activity, three supers high, forming an efficient "honey-production" machine. The hive consists of one queen, many of her workers (female) and some drones (male). With its inhabitants working together as one unit, the hive is considered a superorganism, in which physiological properties of a single organism are executed by its members. For instance, honey bees have a division of labor based on age, in which the younger bees feed the larva, and older house bees will groom each other (mimicking a circulatory system).

Every single person will gleefully point out that hives produce honey, and all will solemnly offer that the honey bees defend themselves with their stingers. These, too, are aspects of the hive as a superorganism.

Due to the widespread media attention to hive decline, everyone is now aware that pesticides and habitat loss are major issues impacting hive health, food security, and they most genuinely want to do something to reduce hive mortality. In order to understand how a superorganism survives in an ecosystem, I start with a fundamental principle: every hive is a collection of chemicals interacting with internal and external chemicals. Everything I do with

THE SUPERORGANISM

A superorganism was defined by W.B. Cannon (1932) as "a mammal with many parts." Here several ways in which a hive's individuals function as one "mammal":

- The regulation of temperature in the brood area
- The division of labor to maximize security of the unit, reduce stress
- The ability to reduce reproduction to a few selected individuals
- The ability to overwinter
- The ability to reproduce by swarming (i.e., division)
- The ability to process food

pollinator habitat, whether on surface mine sites or right-of-way areas or even in my own garden, comes back to seeing the hive as a complex interaction of chemicals. Is the apiary close to a field in bloom? Great, I may not need to wear a full suit. Has a bear attacked a hive? If so, I better have the smoker lit and a full suit. Has a drought caused the bees to begin robbing? I simply wait for another day. All of these examples indicate how a hive responds to environmental, chemical cues, and my success as a beekeeper depends on being sensitive to them.

Because the hive is smaller in population in the winter, I find it easier to start this chapter with the winter season when there are fewer floral resources and the winter cluster is still intact. One of the most frequent questions I receive as the State Apiarist (other than how many times have I been stung) is, "what do the bees do in winter?" Many people, transferring their knowledge of bears, assume that hives go dormant.

Instead, an intriguing phenomenon happens in which a hive of honey bees will have downsized from its summer peak population of 70,000 to around approximately 20,000 adult bees, forming a "winter cluster" as the temperatures consistently fall below 65°F, typically late November in the Ohio and Tennessee Valleys. While there are several aspects of a honey bee hive that illustrate how a super-organism survives, the winter cluster is my favorite.

Hacker's Honey Apiary. 2018.

A winter cluster is unusual in the insect world because it maintains a consistent temperature between 55°F-95°F inside the hive even as external temperatures drop. According to Dewey Caron, the lowest temperature that a colony can survive depends on food availability and the number of bees. When bee brood is present, the internal temperature will be in the upper ranges. Even more unusual is when the colony is broodless, when there is no eggs, larva, pupa, the adult generation will maintain consistent heat, with the center being around 70°F and the outer ranges being around 54°F. Compared to the bumble bee colony, in which only the queen bee

Frame of bees taken with an infrared camera showing heat generating from the winter cluster. 2017.

survives the winter, a honey bee hive will emerge from winter with a mated queen and a cadre of adult workers, ready to start a new generation.

The advantages of this "nest homeostasis" is that the hive will have a good population to rear young brood as the spring temperatures continue to warm. The cluster can defend its queen if mice try to move into the nest. The adult population "at ready" reduces the stress to "make a new generation" again once the temperatures warm. As USDA researcher Dr. Gloria diGrandi-Hoffman says, "It takes a lot of bees to rear a lot of bees." A winter cluster provides just that: a lot of bees at a time of the year when resources are scarce and temperatures unpredictable. Even though the adult bees need resources through the winter, a winter cluster is, in many ways, a safety blanket, insulating a hive from stresses that would normally kill it. Furthermore, a winter cluster is not simply a mass of indistinguishable bees, but rather a densely-layered orb, with the outer layer comprised primarily of older worker bees forming a mantle. As the external temperatures begin to drop, the "mantle" bees interlace their thoracic hair together effectively blocking heat from escaping the hive. The younger bees inside the cluster disperse this heat by relaxing and moving around the frames, provided there are enough nutrition resources for the cluster to consume and generate heat. The winter cluster maintains this consistency in three ways, author William Hesbach writes. "First by conduction because they are touching, then by radiant heat from bees nearby, and finally, with convection via air movement."[4] When bees cluster together and shiver, the heat they generate reaches down to the core, and the younger bees distribute, with their activity, heat back to the mantle bees.

[4]William Hesbach, "Winter Management," *Bee Culture*, Oct. 21, 2016. https://www.beeculture.com/winter-management/

L: This hive has "run out of fuel," to quote Jurgen Tautz, *The Buzz About Bees*. These bees are dead, with their heads buried in the bottom of the cell searching for honey (carbohydrates). L. Steidel. R: Forager bee returning the hive in February 2018 with pollen.

If external temperatures drop below 23°F, then the winter cluster will cease contraction and begin to generate heat by consuming more honey. If the hive goes into winter with too few bees, the hive may die as a result, explains researchers Brian Dennis and William Kemp, comparing the hive to a "hotel with too few staff."[5] Mark Winston explains the baffling phenomena of a beekeeper opening a hive only to hear silence and see worker bees have perished with their heads in the cells searching for honey. "If conditions are too cold, colonies can die even with substantial honey reserves because workers are unable to leave the cluster to get to honey located at the nest periphery."[6] The minimum temperature of the winter cluster in the center is 55°F, which maintains the temperature of the outer shell at 46°F, the minimum temperature required for worker bees to cling to the cluster.[7] So, in effect, the winter bees "jog in place," in the words of Dr. Jim Tew, through the mercurial weather patterns from November to April.[8]

Then, as the days become longer and plants respond to increasing daylight by producing pollen, the winter cluster disperses in search of nutrients and perform "housecleaning" for the hive. With incoming pollen as a trigger to the workers that nutrition is available, the queen will begin to lay eggs. The worker bees will begin to process pollen via anaerobic fermentation into a protein-rich substance known as bee bread, a substance of pollen that has been packed in the bottom of wax cells, mixed with small amounts of nectar and then sealed in cells close to brood.[9] The nectar that is available is quickly collected and processed into honey or used immediately as carbohydrates. In order to survive a full calendar year, every movable-frame beehive needs, on

[5]University of Idaho. "Honeybee hive collapse mystery rooted in hive size." ScienceDaily. ScienceDaily, 24 February 2016. www.sciencedaily.com/releases/2016/02/160224151445.htm
[6]Mark Winston, *The Biology of the Honey Bee*, Harvard UP, 117.
[7]Ibid, 118.
[8]Dr. Jim Tew, "Overwintering Hives," Kentucky State Beekeepers Association, Shepherdsville, KY, Nov. 9, 2018.
[9]Frederick Lee, et al., "Saccharide breakdown and fermentation by the honey bee gut microbiome," Environmental Microbiology, 2014. "The process by which bee bread matures is relatively poorly understood.

UL: This frame shows cells that are beginning to be used as locations for bee bread. The bees chew the pollen grains with their mandibles, add some honey and saliva, the mixture ferments with anaerobic fermentation, and is stored for when the hive needs protein. 2018. UR: This frame shows uncapped nectar, capped honey, and as an extra bonus, a picture of a queen bee. 2018. (Continues on next page)

Photo captions from previous page (continued):
ML: A full frame of capped honey, being samples. 2018. K. Black
MR: A full frame of bee bread. Bee bread created from flower pollen provides protein to hon-
ey bees and other pollinators. It takes an enormous amount of energy for a flowering plant to
produce pollen. Each hive needs about 35-60 pounds of pollen throughout a full year. 2016.
LL: Floral nectar guides shown in a purple coneflower, with a darker center, striated petals,
lavender and purple colors so that bees with UV vision can see the petals, and tall stalks.
LR: Partridge pea nectary. 2014. T.C. Davis.

average, 252 million flowers to produce pollen and nectar.[10] Mark Winston
explained the "flower field math" in *The Biology of the Honey Bee*. "Worker
bees must make one million trips annually to collect pollen, and almost four
million trips to collect nectar." These flowers will provide the "fuel" that the
winter cluster will consume through the winter.[11] A hive will need approximately 126 pounds of honey to exist a full calendar year (60 pounds through
the winter and spring, 60 through the summer and fall). In addition, the hive
will need approximately 35-60 pounds of pollen to process into bee bread.

Unlike wasps, which obtain nutrition by consuming other insects and spiders,
honey bees derive all of their nutrients from flowers. Since honey bees and
flowers co-evolved together, flowers have strategies for attracting pollinators
to them: petal structure, floral scent, colors, and bloom times. It is relatively
easy for a flower to provide nectar, needing only sunlight to photosynthesize
carbon dioxide and water to produce glucose and oxygen. Glucose converts
into sap that travels through the phloem tissue for storage and to become nectar used to attract pollinators. Some flowers have nectaries that have specific
times in which they produce nectar: buckwheat tends to produce nectar in
the morning; sunflowers in the afternoon. Regardless of the time it is available, generally speaking, nectar is an easy "bait" a flower produces in order
to lure a bee to it.

As a forager bee collects nectar, she will add enzymes to the nectar as it is
stored in her honey crop for passage to the hive. Once she has returned to
the hive, she will share her load with a fellow sister. If the hive needs the
forager's nectar, she will be able to distribute her contents among many sister
bees. However, if the quality of the nectar is not good, if there is no place to
store the nectar, or if there is not enough house bees to distribute it, then she
may find it more difficult to share. In her book, *Two Million Blossoms*, author
Kirsten Traynor creates an unforgettable image of how worker bees "actively
dry down the nectar, fanning out a nectar drop repeatedly in their mouth-
parts, like a woman opening and closing a pocket fan."[12]

In contrast to the easy production of nectar, flowering plants have to invest
enormous resources to provide pollen. Plants need phosphorus and nitrogen

[10] I first heard this number from a lecture given by Dr. Jim Tew, Ohio State University, Wooster, Ohio,
March 8, 2015. Mark Winston, *The Biology of the Honey Bee*, Harvard UP, 177.
[11] Jurgen Tautz, *The Buzz About Bees: Biology of a Superorganism*, 216.
[12] Kirsten Traynor, *Two Million Blossoms: Discovering the Medicinal Benefits of Honey*, Middletown, MD,
Image Design Pub, 2011, 55.

Comb with eggs. L. Connor. 2015.

to produce pollen. Prior to industrial agriculture, phosphorus and nitrogen were in short supply in unmanaged lands. As a result, unlike producing copious amounts of nectar, flowering plants produce a limited amount of pollen, especially compared to wind-pollinated plants. Some flowering trees such as sourwood only produce a few grains of pollen, compared to a tree species that does not require insects to function as pollinators, such as pines or elms, which produce copious amounts of pollen carried by the wind. In addition, the pollen grains from flowering species often may be sticky, in order to increase the chances of the grain adhering to a pollinator's body or basket.

Pollen grains have fundamentally different shapes, depending on their species, and so unique and specific to the flower species that the pollen grains are considered to be the "fingerprint" of a flower. These different shapes also help the pollen grains "stick" to a pollinator either on its hair or on its back legs. A basic definition of pollen is provided by one of the pioneers in palynology named Robert Tschudy, in *Aspects of Palynology*. "The function of pollen grains is to accomplish the transport of the male gametophyte to the female flower so that fertilization can take place." [13] Given the hazards of such pollinator-travel, a pollen grain has an "exine" that provides three functions. "It services to protect the protoplasm from excessive dessication and mechanical injury, it provides for the emergence of the pollen tube at the

[13]Robert Tschudy and Richard Scott, "Morphological Description of Spores and Pollen," *Aspects of Palynology*, (1969), 17. Palynology is the counting of different pollen grains (trees or forbs) preserved in peat deposits or lake or river sediments. Melissopalynology is the analysis of pollen grains preserved in honey. In this document, I will refer to Dr. Vaughn Bryant's honey analysis reports from Texas A&M, and also his former student, Dr. Jen O'Keefe at Morehead State University.

time of fertilization, and it provides for size accommodation as the grain loses or absorbs moisture with changing humidity."

While the pollen grain has evolved to help with the flowering plant's ability to reproduce, its impact on the hive is what primarily concerns us in this manuscript. Pollen is rich in protein, along with amino acids that are the building blocks of protein. Pollen that the foragers bring back to the hive typically have at least ten amino acids that are essential for honey bee development: arginine, histidine, lysine, tryptophan, phenylalaine, methionine, threonine, leucine, isoleucine, and valine, according to Dr. Clarence Collison in *Pollen Quality*. If there is a plentiful supply of protein in the form of pollen grains, the queen will begin to lay eggs. If there is a dearth of protein in the form of pollen, the queen will cease brood production. The hive will respond to the lack of pollen by having the foragers increase "the gross amount of pollen returned to the colony, rather than by specializing in collecting pollen with greater protein content," according to Clarence Collison.[14]

Honey bees and humans are the only two species that must process our food, explained University of Illinois professor Dr. May Berenbaum in a lecture I attended in 2018.[15] Given the complex structure of a pollen grain described by Dr. Tschudy, it is no surprise that honey bees cannot digest the pollen grains directly in the field, although other bee species such as bumble bees can consume pollen directly from a flower. The forager bees return with pollen grains adhered to their pollen baskets, their bodies, their antennae, even their eyes!

The foragers deposit their load into beeswax cells, at which point, the nest workers begin the task of converting the pollen grains into bee bread. The nest workers add honey, saliva, and together with fungi, it ferments anaerobically to break down the pollen pellets into bee bread, which can be stored for a long time. However, much remains to be learned about pollen and bee bread. For such an essential hive product as bee bread, there is much to be learned about this substance. Dr. Collison summarizes the need for more research in this way: "Although pollen is the major dietary source of protein, lipids and vitamins for adult worker honey bees, relatively little is known about the mechanism(s) employed by adult worker bees to release the protoplasmic nutrients from the pollen's relatively indigestible cellulose wall (exine)."[16]

Even more to the point: while beekeepers often have some ideas of how much honey is in the hive because of the weight of the "honey super," few beekeepers know how much pollen is in the hive. Pollen is critical to having healthy brood, and shortages of it will mean a decrease in quality brood and, in particular, drones.

[14]Clarence Collison, *Bee Culture*, 2016.

[15]May Berenbaum, lecture, University of Illinois Short Course, Bloomington, Illinois, April 7, 2018.

[16]Clarence Collison, Pollen Consumption and Digestion," *Bee Culture*, Feb. 16, 2017. https://www.beeculture.com/a-closer-look-7/

Frame of brood. 2018.

As the hive transitions from winter to spring and summer, the honey bees thermoregulate the brood nest more stringently. The brood will be damaged if temperatures are too hot or too cold. So as the hive transitions to spring, a majority of the worker bees will be engaged as "heater" bees or "feeder" bees, devoted to keeping the brood warm until the population reaches a healthy 40-50,000 bees.

Once the hive reaches that population of 40,000 bees (still not peak population, mind you), approximately half of the worker bees will specialize in "house" tasks, keeping the brood nest the proper temperature, and half will become foragers. That population epitomizes the hive's most efficient numbers to rear young brood in a temperature-controlled setting and make honey for the following generations. Healthy hives need at least 40,000 workers throughout the year with access to diverse, three-season bloom in order to be productive colonies.

When my grandfather was harvesting honey from log "gums" as a child in Eastern Kentucky, he took for granted the availability of abundant flowers to provide nectar and pollen. However, the "new normal" for 21st century beekeepers is massive land use changes that have reduced or obliterated the flowers available and/or in some cases, have rendered the flowers useless (as in tank mixes).

It is worth mentioning that even in the best of circumstances, not every hive will have enough floral resources to generate 120 pounds of honey or the

Bee "gum." 2017.

35-60 pounds of pollen it will need to survive a year.[17] Dr. Mark Winston cautions: "Although the workers in strong colonies can make up to 163,000 trips daily under ideal conditions, most feral colonies barely collect enough resources to survive, and many colonies starve to death every winter."[18] Dr. Tom Seeley concurs, writing in *Honeybee Democracy* that he "found that less than 25 percent of the "founder colonies" (ones newly started by swarms) would be alive the following spring. In contrast, almost 80 percent of the "established" colonies (ones already in residence for at least a year) would survive winter, no doubt because they hadn't had to start from scratch the previous summer."[19] Similarly, in a separate lecture, University of Georgia professor Dr. Keith Delaplane once explained that only one in four swarms will survive once the bees leave their hive.[20]

The low survival rate may be due to the advent of small hive beetles, which are quick to take advantage of hives with reduced bee populations. Or a hive can go queenless at any time of the year, especially the spring. It can fall victim to disease or vandals. Varroa mites still continue to be the biggest challenge to beekeepers, and I stress to beekeepers that it does very little good to spend a year investing time and money into converting land to pollinator habitat, if the beekeepers do not monitor varroa mite populations on their bees. A varroa mite is an obligate parasite, it has to live on the bodies of honey bees. If the varroa mite loads are higher than three varroa mites per hundred bees, then to quote Jerry Hayes[20.1], "the hive is dead and doesn't even know it yet."

[17]Clarence Collison, "Pollen Quality," *Bee Culture*, April 23, 2016. https://www.beeculture.com/pollen-quality/
[18]Winston, 177.
[19]Tom Seeley, *Honeybee Democracy*, Princeton UP, 2010, 35.
[20]Keith Delaplane, Kentucky State Beekeepers Association Fall Meeting, Somerset, 2009.

Reproductive swarm with a queen and a select group of older workers leave a hive only after scout bees have selected an alternative place to go. Many swarms will go the same vicinity or the same tree year after year. May 6, 2018.

However, all other factors considered, forests represent large areas of bee forage that are removed from agricultural and urban chemicals. This is not a new idea. In 1986, North Carolina professor Arnold Krochmal quoted The U.S. Department of Agriculture's *Beekeeping in the United States* that was published in 1980. This document specifically recommended beekeeping to receive "greater consideration than it now receives in land-use planning, and in providing beekeeping sanctuaries on State and Federal Lands."[21] Prior to the USDA publishing this document, Congress had passed The Multiple Use-Sustained Yield Act of 1960 (MUSYA), which gave the Forest Service authority to administer national forests "for outdoor recreation, range, timber, watershed, and wildlife and fish purposes." Twenty years later, Arnold Krochmal vents in his article, "There has been no response to this urgent need for an industry which covers the contiguous states as well as Hawaii."

In an overview of forestry history, Doug McCleary concurs with Krochmal. "In 1974, the Forest and Rangelands Renewable Resources Planning Act (RPA) required the Forest Service periodically to assess the national long-term

[20.1]Personal communication, Vice President, North America, Vita Bee Health; author of "The Classroom" in the *American Bee Journal*.
[21]Arnold Krochmal, "Forests as Nectar Sources," *Bee Culture* 114.12 (1986), 640.

Hiving a swarm. While swarms can seem random to people, "Almost always a swarm selects the single best site from among the dozen or more possible homesites that its scout bees have discovered," according to Tom Seeley. "Swarms make calculated decisions about where to relocate, a type of "democracy," according to Tom Seeley in *Honeybee Democracy*. "The better the site, the stronger the dances advertising it, hence the greater the positive feedback for this site," he summarizes (226-227). May 6, 2018.

demand and supply situation for all renewable resources, and to plan how agency programs would address projected resource demands and needs. In 1976, the National Forest Management Act (NFMA) provided detailed guidelines for the management of national forest lands and for increased participation of the public in national forest decision-making. Both the RPA and NFMA were intended to encourage planning and stakeholder involvement (Fedkiw 1999). It was hoped that the process could help to resolve the differences between environmentalists and timber, mining and livestock-grazing communities. This did not transpire."[22] Furthermore, as of 2019, this plan still has not transpired and explains the current frustration among commercial beekeepers in the western states who still struggle with the Bureau of Land Management and Forest Service officials who refuse to issue permits to commercial beekeepers because of concerns of floral competition between managed honey bees and native bees.

Before reading Arnold Krochmal in 2003, I had never heard of the term, "nectar blocks," in which Krochmal wanted 5% of new plantings to be devoted to a nectar-producing flowering tree. However, his argument for better

---

[22]Doug McCleary, Reinventing the United States Forest Service: Evolution from Custodial Management, to Production Forestry, to Ecosystem Management. http://www.fao.org/3/ai412e/AI412E06.htm

forestry management for beekeepers still resonates today in 2019. Consider his efforts in North Carolina in which he requested the National Forests "consider planting blocks of sourwood, *Oxydendrum arboretum*, perhaps to the amount of 5% of new plantings, were ignored."

An assistant director of the Forest Service explained to Krochmal that beekeeping "isn't part of their mission."

Krochmal's response was withering: "Neither are recreational vehicles," he noted dryly. Citing his experience in Russia, in which he learned "that ¾ of the honey Russian beekeepers produced is said to originate in the forests of Russia, and further, helicopters were used to move colonies to blossoming forests," Krochmal urged beekeepers to attend Forest Service Management meetings to make their needs known. Furthermore, Krochmal suggested that the U.S. Forest Service needs to become aware of the role trees play in providing nutrition for all pollinators, not just honey bees. His solution was to recommend that National and State Forests include plantings of selected small blocks of nectar sources from sourwood to basswoods, locusts and others as well.

A few years before Krochmal pursued his efforts in North Carolina, Kentucky forester Patrick Angel, a surface mine inspector at the time, worked with Peabody Coal Mines and Tennessee Valley Authority to set up an apiary on former surface mine site in Madisonville, KY. College students focused on honey production, and for a while, the project was very successful.[23] The project ended due to vandalism.

Some forest-based beekeeping projects have existed internationally, too. When the price of copper dropped in 2005, a Zambia copper mining company Bwana Mkubwa Mining Limited (BMML) donated beekeeping equipment worth about $20 million [about US $4250] to Kansafwe community in Chief Chiwala's area in Ndola [Zambia].[24] In Zambia, at the time of this writing, approximately 95% are bark hives, and a beekeeper has, on average, 70. It has been estimated that there are some 20,000 beekeepers and 6,000 honey hunters in Zambia. At least half of the beekeepers are found in North-Western Province. Traditional bark-hive beekeeping is dominantly a male activity. Women beekeepers are few and have mostly emerged through various project interventions, e.g., to promote the use of top bar hives.[25]

Labor is the factor that prohibits beekeeping, especially for women. Some programs intend to help women beekeepers. However, in an interview with agricultural extension agent Guni Mickels-Kokwe, she carefully explains that

[23]Patrick Angel, and C.M. Christensen. 1976. "Honey Production on Reclaimed Strip Mine Soil." 708-711, in: *Hill Lands: Proceedings of an International Symposium*. West Virginia University, Morgantown.
[24]"Zambia: Bwana Mkubwa Donates Bee-Keeping Kit to Chief Chiwala's Kansafwe," *Times of Zambia*, January 19, 2005.
[25]Guni Mickels-Kokwe. *Small-scale Woodland-based Enterprises with Outstanding Economic Potential: The Case of Honey in Zambia*. Center for International Forestry Research, Bogor Barat, Indonesia, 2006. 47.

A varroa mite on worker honey bee. USDA.

behind the financial aid lie assumptions that do not necessarily hold true when faced with practical beekeeping problems.[26]

Irish Aid, for instance, provided grants for modern hives, but these grants were not as effective as they could have been. The grants were based on assumption: if women cannot go in the forest or climb trees, [Langstroth] hives "fixes" that problem. But Langstroth hives have problems with ants, and given the swarming instinct of African honey bees, the occupancy rate is low. The hives have to be high to access bees. An African "traditional hive" has a cylindrical shape, so it can hang from a branch or be placed on a branch in a tree. Placing a hive high in a tree makes it easier to attract bees at their usual flying height and to protect hives against fire, honey badgers, red ants, and other pests.[27] Beekeeping is never as easy as it seems on paper.

In Mickels-Kokwe's opinion, a better approach is to acknowledge that it is impractical to expect women to climb trees to check hives or even to embrace "movable frame" hives in a location so far removed from hardware stores. If women can be permitted to hire some of the labor of honey harvesting, she suggests, they can use the value-added products of beekeeping to make honey beer, which is a very valuable item with which to barter. Her point: women do not have to be beekeepers to profit from bees. Honey brewery is a full-time occupation, and it is a way of raising labor (pay in food and beer) as well as social entertainment and cohesion.[28]

Guni Nickels-Kokwe hails from Finland. Growing up as a child, she saw how post-WWII Industrial Revolution affected her homeland. The general government consensus was that "land was around, and land can not be moved

[26]On site interview at Apimondia International Congress, Melbourne Australia, Sept. 12, 2007.
[27]Mickels-Kokwe, 12.
[28]Mickels-Kokwe, 44.

around, so the solution was to move people around." The big disadvantage to this form of social reorganization is that education does not necessarily help in these circumstances.

Similarly, she sees a parallel movement in the programs for beekeepers in Zambia. In Northern Zambia, assumptions are not very fixed. "When confronted with proof, ideas can change, [the people] can change" she explains. This is especially important in teaching people about the consequences of deforestation on beekeeping potential in Zambia are far more serious than those of bark-hive harvesting.[29]

In a final analysis that mirrors many beekeeping families in the United States, Mickels-Kokwe explains: "Production is highly individualistic in many Zambian households. It is not uncommon to find that households work together as a production unit, drawing upon the labour of many members of the household. However, when it comes to the marketing sales, these are individualistic, with the husband and wife managing the sales from their individual fields.[30]

As Mickels-Kokwe observed in Finland, the education system does not "help" if rural economies are dependent on land. Similarly in Appalachia, if education programs could focus on forestry, apiculture, and other land-based sciences, then there may be more applicability.

In helping people learn about the crisis impacting pollinators, I have learned how much people have to re-connect with not simply the bees, but also land, sciences, and for that matter, their own family members and communities. For many people, it is easy to embrace the idea of increasing pollinator habitat. Pollinator habitat projects offer gratification when flowers are in bloom, and people do not get stung. Planting flowers or trees does not *seem* to require the labor that managing a beehive requires, although anyone who has tried to remove Johnson grass *(Sorghum halepense)* knows precisely how difficult it can be to remove. The more I worked on surface mine sites, the more I planted flowers and trees in my own suburban yard. I started with container pots of herbs and gradually developed a bigger garden, with room for squash, beans, tomatoes and mustards to provide more variety for diverse bee species (the pumpkin bees, the bumble bees, etc.). The more forage I provided to bees, the more bees of different species benefited. Now there are more mason bee houses than honey bee hives in my yard. My motto has become, "Acre by acre, flower by flower, bee by bee."

[29]Mickels-Kokwe, 19.
[30]Mickels-Kokwe, 64.

CHAPTER TWO: APPALACHIA

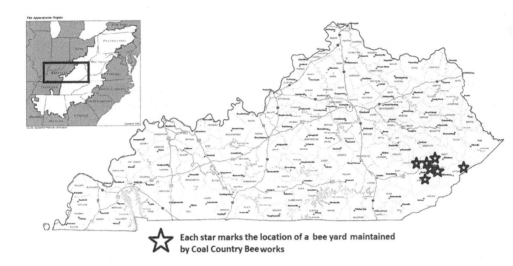

⭐ Each star marks the location of a bee yard maintained by Coal Country Beeworks

Until 2014, Coal Country Beeworks had seven apiaries established in Eastern Kentucky in an effort to establish "honey corridors." The Eastern Kentucky Winter Bee School continues to be held in the month of January, located in Perry County.

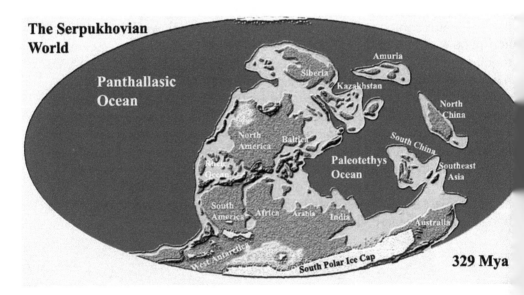

Map of Early Carboniferous period, when tectonic action pushed the continent of Africa into North America, forming the Appalachian Mountains. http://www.scotese.com/earth.htm.

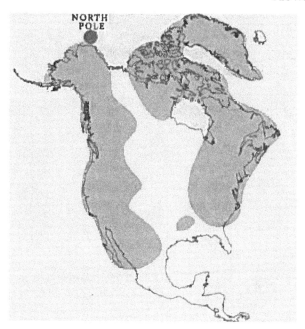

Graphic from Tim Flannery, *The Eternal Frontier: An Ecological History of North America and Its Peoples*. This drawing illustrates how the Appalachian region was separated from the western states by wide, shallow Bearpaw Sea. Flannery refers to Appalachia a "biological island," and it is one reason why the two regions have different flowering species.

On March 21, 1968, the first day of spring equinox, I was born in Sunshine, Kentucky, in Harlan County. Although contemporary writers and pundits have disparaged the Appalachians, I have been mesmerized by its complicated history, starting with its ancient past: the coal formed from huge trees and ferns in the Carboniferous, and the living remnants from that time with quasi-tropical trees such as pawpaws, the tulip poplar (which is in the magnolia family) and rhododendrons. Far from being the land-locked elevated mountain range that it is now, the Appalachians were a lush swamp. The fact that the Appalachians are now a mountain range is a consequence of "Deep Time," when most of the modern continents traveled over most of the world, splitting from old neighbors and joining to others as if in a global square dance," explains Colin Tudge, in *The Time Before History*.[31]

Formed over 450 million years ago in the Late Carboniferous and Permian, the eastern and southern margins of North America collided with Africa and South America, producing a great mountain belt from the Appalachians to the Southern Rockies with the Bearpaw Sea in the middle. In effect, geographer Daniel Prothero explains, North America was two biological "islands," the Appalachians linked the eastern "island" from Newfoundland to Mexico, and it was relatively stable. On the other side, America's "western island"

[31]Colin Tudge, *The Time Before History: 5 Million Years of Human Impact*, Scribners, 1996, 48.

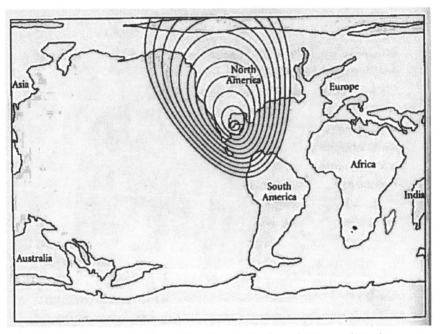

Graphic from Tim Flannery, *The Eternal Frontier: An Ecological History of North America and Its Peoples.* This graphic illustrates how North America was impacted by the asteroid that hit Chicxulub."The nearer the impact point," Flannery writes, "the more likely the devastation was to be total. Seen this way, just three locations were sufficiently remote or sheltered to act as a refuge to plants—in the lee of the mountain ranges of the Sierra Nevada and the Appalachians, and far to the north, inside the Arctic Circle". 29.

was a geologically restless land that had been joined to Asia via Beringian land bridge for hundreds of millions of years. Its fauna and flora were largely shared with Asia."[32] In the middle, stretching though the states that are now the Heartland, was the Bearpaw Sea. Although the Bearpaw Sea kept the two islands distinct, "North America was created differently [than other continents]—it resulted from a victory of the forces of union."[33]

Trees and plants did well in Appalachia during the Carboniferous. The dominant species of tree, the *Lepidodendron*, could grow up to 175 feet as long as water was available. Without water, according to author Barbara Freese of *Coal: A Human History*, "These proud giants of the paleoforest would have weakened, sagged, and finally collapsed under their own weight."[34]

Insects also grew to mammoth proportions. "Cockroaches reached a foot in length, the dragonflies had wing-spans of up to thirty inches, and the millipedes reached six feet in length—as long as a cow," writes Barbara Freese quoting David Attenborough.

Some plants and insects such as bees managed to survive an asteroid impact at 65 million years ago near Chicxulub, Mexico, even though other species

---

[32]Daniel Prothero, *Evolution of the Earth*, McGraw-Hill, 2003.

[33]Tim Flannery, *The Eternal Frontier*, 10.

[34]Barbara Freese, *Coal: A Human History*, 18-19.

such as dinosaurs and the large cats went extinct in North America. Since the eastern side of North America was semi-tropical, the plants evolved with the solitary pollinators such as tomatoes, pumpkins, squash, and cucumbers. Trees such as sugar maples and pawpaws produced sweeteners or sweet fruit. Other types of plants such as maize and beans were wind-pollinated or solitary-insect pollinated. However, many plants ended up as coal because "they failed to decay the way plants usually do," Freese says. "Normally when a plant dies, oxygen penetrates its cells and decomposes it into carbon dioxide and water. As the dense mass of Carboniferous plants died, though, they often fell into oxygen-poor water or mud, or were covered by other dead plants or sediments."[35] The plants only partly decayed, leaving behind massive seams of black carbon, "buried sunshine," the "Devil's excrement," and other euphemisms.[36]

Even as plants and pollinators were stabilizing in the Appalachian region, North America itself was far from static. North America was just beginning another round of change beginning in the late Cretaceous time period when the dormant Precambian "basement floor" in the West began to come to life beneath the wide seas and marsh lands. As the basement floor began to lift, the seas drained to the Gulf of Mexico and the Arctic Ocean. Then, to quote geologist Dave Love, in John McPhee's *Rising from the Plains*, "All hell broke loose."[37]

To read John McPhee's account, the crustal sheets detached themselves and went sliding eastward over much younger rocks. He lists five mountain ranges, such as the Bighorns, the Beartooths, the Sierra Madre, the Medicine Bows, the Washakies, and more that formed very rapidly in geologic time. Geologists refer to this event as the Laramide Revolution. McPhee's summary sentence is, "It was as if mountains had appeared in Ohio, inboard of the Appalachian thrust sheets, like a family of hogs waking up beneath a large blanket." Erosion continued to erode the Appalachians, a time when "everything went blah," in the words of geologist David Love, even as the Western states continued to deal with volcanic fissures and other tectonic activities.[38]

That is, until Australia unzipped itself from Antarctic, a tectonic move that would change the world's climate forever, in the Oligocene. It is beyond the scope of this book to describe in geologic detail the enormous changes that happened as a result of Oligocene, but the resulting altitude and aridity differences meant that forest tree species in North America such as figs and magnolias gave way to maples, oaks, and beeches.

[35]Freese 20.
[36]Richard Rhodes, "Nuclear Option," *The New York Times Book Review*, Feb. 10, 2019, 15.
[37]John McPhee, *Rising from the Plains*, 1986, 48.
[38]McPhee, 50.

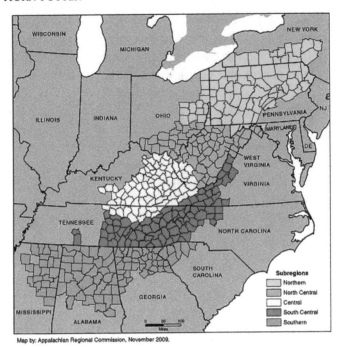

Map by: Appalachian Regional Commission, November 2009.

Map of the Appalachian Sub-Regions, taken from the Appalachian Regional Commission website: https://www.arc.gov/research/MapsofAppalachia.asp?MAP_ID=31

Eastern Kentucky is part of a region known as Central Appalachia. As a rule, to borrow from historian Walter Prescott Webb's scholarship, its civilization has stood on three legs—land, water, and timber.[39] On the surface, it is defined by its mesophytic forest that covers 54 mountainous counties of diverse flowering tree species, some of which contribute to excellent varietal honeys.[40] These species include but are not limited to a variety of maples, willows, tulip poplar, black locust, basswood, sourwood, and understory trees such as serviceberry, dogwoods, and redbud. Even shrubs such as sumac and understory trees such as witch hazel provide bloom into the autumn.

But it was the coal underneath that catapulted the region to the forefront of the nation's energy sector for over a century. The Appalachian region has

[39]Walter Prescott Webb, *The Great Plains,* 1951. To quote Webb: "At [the 98th meridian] fault, the ways of life and of living changed. Practically every institution that was carried across it was either broken and remade or else greatly altered. When people first crossed this line they did not immediately realize the imperceptible change that had taken place in their environment, nor, more is the tragedy, did they foresee the full consequences which that change was to bring in their own characters and in their modes of life...Their plight has been stated in this way: east of the Mississippi civilization stood on three legs— land, water, and timber; west of the Mississippi not one but two of these legs were withdrawn—water and timber—and civilization was left on one leg—timber, 9.
[40]The Central Appalachian region consists of Eastern Kentucky, Eastern Tennessee, West Virginia, Western Pennsylvania, the western part of Virginia. Mesophytic forests are those that are in temperate climate, with rainfall, and not too adverse conditions. According to Chester Arnold's, "The Fossil Plant Record," the mesophytic forests responded to changing conditions: "The summers became drier, though rainfall in general was not deficient, and seasonal changes became more pronounced" in the Miocene Epoch. *Aspects of Palynology: An Introduction to Plant Microfossils in Time.* Eds: Robert Tschudy and Richard Scott. New York: Wiley Interscience, 1969, 139.

Great Culebra Cut. https://commons.wikimedia.org/wiki/File:The_Panama_Canal_--_The_Great_Culebra_Cut.jpg

been a center of coal mining, providing as much as fifty percent of the nation's electricity and helping power the U.S. economic expansion for much of the 20th century. "Coal was no mere fuel," writes Freese, "and no mere article of commerce. It represented humanity's triumph over nature—the foundation of civilization itself. As another writer put it, "With Coal, we have light, strength, power, wealth, and civilization; without Coal, we have darkness, weakness, poverty, and barbarism."[41]

Coal still provides much of the electricity in Kentucky, West Virginia and Wyoming, although many underground coal mines have closed because the seams have been mined, methane gas levels are too high underground, or a coal company realizes it is cheaper to surface mine the shallower seams nearer the top of a mountain. In "Mapping how the United States Generates Its Electricity," John Muyskens, Dan Keating and Samuel Granados provides an excellent state-by-state map in *The Washington Post,* charting the diverse energy grid.[42]

Surface mining technology is not new; it is a by-product of large-scale engineering and technology derived and developed from the Panama Canal in the 1880s. An ambitious artificial waterway, the Panama Canal allowed ships to sail from the Atlantic to the Pacific (and vice versa) without having to sail around Cape Horn. Borrowing from military technology, engineers developed various extractive and excavation technologies to remove rock, control water, create lifts for ships, and arrange artificial lakes. One example is the

[41]Freese, 10.

[42]John Muyskens, Dan Keating and Samuel Granados, "Mapping how the United States Generates Its Electricity, *The Washington Post*, March 28, 2017. http://wapo.st/power-plants?tid=ss_mail

Culebra Cut, formally known as the Gailliard Cut, that cuts through the Continental Divide in Panama to form an artificial valley. Started by the French, but then transferred to the U.S. in 1904, this cut connected the ships coming from the Atlantic to the largest manmade lake at the time, Gatun Lake, so that the ships can continue to the Gulf of Panama (and then to the Pacific). These engineering feats transferred to the coal mining regions of Appalachia, the Rockies, anywhere that minerals and fossil fuels could be extracted.

While extractive industry is not new, what *is* new is that citizens are demanding more environmental protections. Extractive industry technology has tended to outpace legislation for miner safety and/or reclamation. The United States excels at developing the technology to do extractive mining; it lags, however, in the costs associated with safety and a reduction of the impact of mining on the environment, such as stream protection measures or air quality regulations. With natural gas becoming a predominant fuel for electricity in the United States, an emerging trend is to improve reclamation in Central Appalachia. Safety regulations have increased oversight since the Upper Big Branch mine disaster, in which twenty-nine miners were killed in April 5, 2010, in West Virginia.[43] Reforestation brings added opportunities because it can promote several economies too.

The floral opportunities for beekeepers on surface mine sites in Central Appalachia never have been properly documented. In my opinion, this is a flaw with how the reclamation process was first defined by Office of Surface Mining. In its list of post-mine land uses, which has been driven by the potential for taxable income, the priorities are commercial development, then civic project developments such as schools, and last are forests, parks and "other natural wastelands."[44]

Yet, when it comes time to consider the options for reclamation, reforestation is much cheaper for mine owners to consider than commercial options, such as trying to lure a prospective factory, prison, or neighborhood developer to build on a surface mine site once the coal has been extracted. As coal company officials consult with landowners on how the landowners would like their land reclaimed for post-mine land use, instead of simply opting for pasture, landowners may now consider a wide variety of pollinator habitat meadow mixes or planting trees.

---

[43]Don Blankenship, the CEO of Massey Energy, a company that once mined 40 million tons of coal a year and employed 6000 people, spent one year in jail for the 29 miners who died a mine that had numerous safety flaws. He was found guilty of conspiracy to violate safety standards. "We haven't had a coal dust explosion in 20 years," said Celeste Monforton, a former M.S.H.A. policy adviser who now teaches at George Washington University. "They are completely preventable, and everybody knows it. Coal dust explosions happen in the Ukraine and China. Not the United States." D. Segal, NY Times, 21 June 15.

[44]Interview with Dr. Don Graves, retired forestry professor, Feb. 2007. Starfire site, Perry County, KY.

An Appalachian Regional Reforestation Initiative Arbor Day event, showing the site with a 20-degree slope and loose compaction. OSMRE staff. 2012.

Appalachian trees grow really well on rocky slopes with poor soils, even after disturbance, if compaction is reduced. When surface mining was just getting started in the 1960s, a type of mining known as "shoot and shove" would allow miners to access coal, and the forests would re-seed itself very quickly. When one visits some of these "shoot and shove" areas, one is hard-pressed to tell the difference where mining had taken place. The forest canopy has grown so thick, an observer would have to know where the site was.

However, the floods and erosion could have horrible impacts on the people living in the region. So, the 1977 Surface Mining Control and Reclamation Act meant more federal oversight of surface mine sites. As previously discussed, too much compaction of surface mine soil had unexpected consequences, namely that native trees had difficulty establishing root systems. After twenty years of a type of reclamation that resulted in "pastoral" areas, the Appalachian Regional Reforestation Initiative foresters worked with Office of Surface Mining Reclamation and Enforcement (OSMRE) Officials to modify 1977 Surface Mining Control and Reclamation Act laws so that compaction can be reduced.

There are four main steps to prepping a site for an ARRI tree planting on an active surface mine site:

• Trees grow better on a slope, so there is at least a 20-degree contour. The steeper the contour, the better trees will grow, but due to concerns about flooding and erosion, OSMRE has been reluctant to increase the contour for surface mine sites.

• The site has less compaction as previous sites used to have. The reduced compaction helps bare root seedlings trees establish their root systems more quickly.

• Trees need to have market value, preferably "high value" hardwoods, but in recent years, understory trees have been defined as having important value to birds, bats, and pollinators.

• Fourth, an ARRI reforestation site is prepped with 4-feet of topsoil, compromised of loose mine soils free of pathogenic microbial communities such as *Phytophthora* root rot, which has hindered American chestnut (*Castanea dentata*) and other reclamation research. This topsoil is actually deeper than many existing topsoil areas for Appalachian forests. Thus, many bare-root seedlings get a "head-start" if they are planted with this much soil.

If a property owner owns a former surface mine site, I recommend that the landowner reach out to the nonprofit called Green Forests Work that derived from Appalachian Regional Reforestation Initiative. This nonprofit identifies legacy sites and "rips" compacted soil that prevents trees from growing. When a property is "ripped," a huge Caterpillar track-type tractor called a D-9 (or a newer model called a D-10) arrives at the site with a large pick attached. This pick will plow through the compacted soil, creating straight furrows in the flattened land. Sometimes, if there are enough funds to pay the driver and

L: A professional tree planter. M. Sharp, 2012.
R: A bucket of trees. Prior to a planting event, Green Forests Work staff will set out buckets of trees, filled with mixed species, including good pollen and nectar-producing trees. Teams will pair up and plant these bare-root seedlings once the soil has been "ripped." 2019.

A bare root seedling, properly planted on loose "spoil." C. Radcliffe. 2008.

the gasoline required to run it, the property will be "cross-ripped" (furrows created that go across the ripped furrows) just to provide more uncompacted soil for tree roots to expand.

Then, a professional tree crew, or a volunteer group, or both, will plant bare-root seedlings. The average cost to "rip" a 5-acre plot for reforestation was about $25,000 in 2012.

Typically, the best season to plant bare-root tree seedlings will be from November through February. Some states may extend the tree planting season as late as Arbor Day (April) since tree-planting events make great community events and good public relations. Some of these trees will survive. But generally, the warmer the weather, the worse for the bare-root seedlings that are planted. Large-scale industries that are reviewed by federal oversight and/ or answer to stakeholders must consider the proper tree planting season because if the trees do not survive, the company will have to buy more trees, hire more tree planters, deal with more issues such as flooding and erosion. Since mine sites are "graded" by inspectors for the survival rate of these trees, mine operators want the tree seedlings to survive. The higher the tree survival rate, the less expensive it is to have to have a tree crew come in and replant.

Also, if a landowner simply wants to buy a former mine site after the land has been released by the federal inspectors, he or she may simply consult with local Natural Resource Conservation Service agents, especially if land parcels are smaller acreages. There are now NRCS Pollinator Handbooks for Kentucky and West Virginia, resources that became available in 2016 and 2017.

A Caterpillar D-9, ripping compacted soil prior to a reforestation event. Courtesy of Green Forests Work, LLC. 2018.

A landowner who is not trying to plant large-scale acreage may want to opt to plant ball-and-burlap trees, which are older and better able to handle the stress of being transplanted. Another option is for a landowner to simply hand-collect seed from trees such as sourwood and then hand-scatter the seeds on bare soil. Sourwood trees (*Oxydendrum arboretum*) do not do well at all in being transplanted. Yet, this same species will volunteer very easily via seed. With this type of tree, which is a slow grower and not "conducive" to the type of reforestation programs in place by the Office of Surface Mining,

Professional tree crew planting in Perry County, KY. M. Sharp. 2012.

I recommend people simply collect by hand the seed and scatter plentiful-ly on bare ground if possible The point: not all species abide by Office of Surface Mining polices. Not all land areas are the same. People need to be flexible and work with the tree species that are unique to the region.

The Appalachian economy has been in decline since the Great Recession of 2008. Predicted for years, the decline in coal has turned out to be vast natural gas reserves that have weaned energy companies away from fossil fuels, not politicians and their policies. Even so, the void left by the decline in coal mining has created opportunities for beekeepers. The idea behind Coal Country Beeworks, a university-based extension program focused on apiculture, was a simple two-pronged approach: Unemployed people could be trained to plant trees in the fall and winter, and then keep bees from spring to fall.

As invasive autumn olive (*Elaeagnus umbellata*) spreads, this region needs to eradicate it and other invasive species as well as plant diverse tree species that had existed prior to mining. Furthermore, there is need for domestic hon-ey. Every year, the U.S. imports 400 million pounds of honey from interna-tional sources, some of which has been contaminated with chloramphenicol and other adulterants. In addition, the United States imports beeswax from Africa because domestic beeswax has too many contaminants for the cos-metic industry. The Appalachian region could offset these commodity needs if people can be employed to work seasonally: tree planters in fall and winter, and beekeepers during spring and summer. To circle back to Walter Prescott Webb's explanation of civilizations east of the Mississippi River, instead of the Appalachian civilization resting on three legs (land, water and timber), it could rest on a fourth, apiculture.

Appalachia is not a static region, fixed in time or place. As a primary contrib-utor and leader in industrialization, Appalachia and the rest of the country are creating a vast and untested experiment with the advent of industrial agriculture, a technological landscape, and ten billion people inhabiting the earth. Given the rapid changes to the environment, I think of the geologist Dave Love, describing the mountain-building event 70-80 million years ago, a time he said when "all hell broke loose." If we in the Appalachian region heed the lessons of Deep Time, we will consider how best to take care of forests because history has shown them to be the buffer zone between a comfortable civilization and mass extinction.

CHAPTER THREE: FLOWERING TREES

When I first started Coal Country Beeworks in 2008, I focused on plant species as much as I did on bees. Because coal mines companies had budgets with line items dedicated to reforestation, I worked with reclamation officers to supplement existing and approved tree lists, suggesting a few flowering tree species to include on mine sites. My strategy was to work within an existing budget if possible and not create a new line item for a company that answers to stakeholders and federal regulators. Bond money is paid by a coal company prior to surface mining. Once a mine has succeeded in reclamation, the bond money is returned to the coal company. If the coal companies must reforest to have their bond monies returned, all pollinators could benefit from the long-term impact of more habitat. If the coal companies would plant more flowering species, the success rate of other species would improve and bond monies could be returned, perhaps much more quickly.

This chapter is not an exhaustive listing of all the flowering trees that produce nectar and pollen in North America. We started with a list of tree species considered "high value" defined by Office of Surface Mining and Reclamation officials. "High value" trees are those with market value, in terms of building houses, making furniture, fencing, telephone poles. However, understory trees are "high value" to beekeepers. In some cases, we were able to change the perception of understory trees.

Kentucky State Biologist Casey Shrader compiled the Kentucky Pollinator Handbook.
Downloaded at:
https://efotg.sc.egov.usda.gov/references/public/KY/KPH5a.pdf

Another noteworthy item about this chapter: I have included, where possible, species in which pollen grains were found in honey samples analyzed by Dr. Jen O'Keefe at Morehead State University or Dr. Vaughn Bryant at Texas A&M. Both O'Keefe and Bryant specialize in a skill known as melissopalynology, i.e., the identification of pollen grains found in honey. The identification and calculation of pollen grains can "type" a honey, informing beekeepers the species and frequency of plants visited by honey bees. As of this point in time, this type of honey analysis is the most economically feasible way to know what flowers the bees visit.[45] According to the International Commission of Bee Biology, if honey is comprised of 46% of one pollen, the beekeeper may market that honey as a varietal honey. For example, if a beekeeper labels a product "clover honey," he or she must have an analysis showing that 46% percent of the pollen grains derive from clover plants.

Many honeys in the Appalachia have such a diverse array of pollens, that it is impossible for many beekeepers to claim their products are monofloral. This is good thing, in my opinion. The forest-based honey in this region is very complex. Although a honey analysis based on pollen is imperfect (such as some pollens can fall off while a bee is in flight, leading to an inaccurate "count," and some plants do not produce much pollen), sending a sample to a lab is the best that many "small-time" beekeepers can do to understand how to label honey for the market correctly. By providing images of the pollen grains along with the tree species in this section, I hope to clarify for both beekeeper and general reader the complexities of honey, the need for better label laws, and immense challenges beekeepers face in educating the consumer about the honey one buys.

Finally, this chapter is arranged seasonally, with flowering tree species discussed in terms of their bloom time, beginning with the earliest spring bloomers to the last of the fall blooming species. This structure may provide readers a botanical "timeline," so they can consider adding a species to their own gardens to fill bloom "gap" or brighten a corner during the fall or perhaps work with a corporation to consider converting an acre of land. Approaching these plants with seasons in mind may help the readers "see" a landscape from the perspective of a honey bee.

WILLOWS (SALIX SPP.)

The "eager beavers of the forest"

Willows are considered vigorous "pioneer" trees, colonizing open ground, and elbowing their way into new terrain, doing well in disturbed soils, such as surface mine sites. There are over 300 varieties of willows, ranging from low shrubs to very tall trees. Black willow (*Salix nigra*), which is native to the Eastern woodlands, is prevalent. Weeping willow (*Salix babylonica*) and pussy willow (*Salix discolor)* are common too.

---

[45]Nuclear magnetic resonance (NMR) analysis is the future of honey analysis but for many beekeepers, this form of testing is cost-prohibitive. Kentucky is currently working toward developing a DNA analysis method as well, and that may be feasible in the next year. So pollen analysis is the most feasible way of helping beekeepers label and market their honey.

In his ground-breaking book, *The Hidden Life of Trees: What They Feel, How They Communicate: Discoveries from a Secret World*, Peter Wohlleben calls pussy willows, the "eager beavers" of the tree world for their ability to out-grow their competitors by three feet or more in the same year. "In just ten years, they can transform land that once lay fallow into a young forest."[46] Their seeds are padded and small and can be carried long distances away from a confined forest environment where large trees already exist. Pioneer trees hate shade, generally speaking, and in Appalachia, willow trees take immediate advantage of more sunlight in the early spring to produce nectar and pollen.

The ability to grow quickly is as much the willows' defense as it is an advantage to stake out new territory. The growth means that the bark will harden, providing a shield against browsing deer and/or bison. In *The Tree: A Natural History of What Trees Are, How They Live and Why They Matter*, Colin Tudge mentions that in some environments, willows "send out underground stems to form vast clones: a wood that, in effect, is a single plant."[47] Much of the willow nectar will be used by the honey bees for spring buildup of the worker bee population. As the hive increases its population to 40,000 workers by March, the hive steadily consumes nectar (carbohydrates) and pollen (protein) from the early spring willows. In *Honey Plants of North America* (1926), John Lovell reports anecdotes of beehives gaining 6-10 pounds of honey in New York, and as much as 100 pounds of black willow honey in Louisiana.[48]

Willows are dioecious, with some trees bearing male flowers, and some trees bearing female flowers. Both produce catkins that honey bees forage. Ideally, "Willows need bees to fly first to the male willows, collect pollen there, and then transport the pollen to the female trees. If it was the other way around," explains Peter Wohlleben in *The Hidden Life of Trees*," "there would be no fertilization."[49] In an effort to attract bees to the male catkins first, the male willows make the catkins extra yellow, a clear visual signal to the bees flying above. "Once the bees have had their first meal of sugary nectar," Wohlleben continues, "they leave and visit the inconspicuous greenish flowers of the female trees."

Other pollinators also benefit from the floral strategies employed by willows, specifically the early-blooming pussy willow (*Salix discolor*). Female bumble bees, the only caste to be flying in early spring, collect their nutrients from

[46]Peter Wohlleben, *The Hidden Life of Trees: What They Feel, How They Communicate: Discoveries from a Secret World*, London, 181. In describing how trees relate to one another in a given area, Wohlleben refers to the term "wood-wide web," first coined by Dr. Suzanne Simard in the article: "Net Transfer of Carbon between Tree Species with Shared Ectomycorrhizal Fungi," *Nature* 388 (1997): 579-82. She and her colleagues discovered that different tree species are in contact with one another, even when they regard each other as competitors (Wohlleben,11).

[47]Tudge *The Tree*,174.

[48]Lovell, Medina, OH, A.I. Root, 234.

[49]Wohlleben, 23-24.

L: Weeping willow (*Salix babylonica*). 2019.
R: Pussy willows (*Salix discolor*), colonizing a space. 2019.

pussy willow.[50] Many species of the native *Andrena* bees (some people call these "miner bees," one of the first native solitary bees to appear in spring) also work pussy willow, primarily for brood-rearing, according to Lovell.[51] Once pussy willows have finished blooming, other species of willows such riverbank willow (*S. longifolia*), silky willow (*S. sericea*), the beaked willow (*S. rostrate*), the heart-shaped willow (*S. cordata*), the white willow (*S. alba*), and the shining willow (*S. lucida*) will bloom, providing for continued sustained sources of nutrition.[52] According to Kentucky biologist and author Shannon Trimboli, "Depending on the species, willows can be either wind or insect pollinated. The wind-pollinated species produce pollen, but no nectar. The insect-pollinated species produce both nectar and pollen."[53]

Even though willows provide an abundance of pollen and nectar, beekeepers tend to be rather oblivious to willows. Few beekeepers have their honey tested, so they may not realize how consistently willow pollen appears in honey analysis reports.[54]

---

[50]Bumble bees are semi-social, which means only the queen will over-winter. There is a caste system in place based on reproductive division of labor. In the early spring, only the queen will emerge from her ground nest to forage: there are no daughters at this point. Once spring arrives and nutrition readily available, the queen will rear daughters, and finally rear males later in the season.
[51]Lovell, 237.
[52]Ibid, 237.
[53]Shannon Trimboli, *Honey Plants in the Ohio Valley*, Solidago Press, 2018, 55.
[54]There are a couple of reasons why beekeepers do not have their honey analyzed: 1. Only a few laboratories that offer the service of melissopalynology; 2. Many beekeepers go on anecdotal observations between the times the flowers are blooming and when honey supers are capped; 3. Many beekeepers are oblivious of the label laws in this country; 4. Consumers do not know to ask for a pollen analysis.

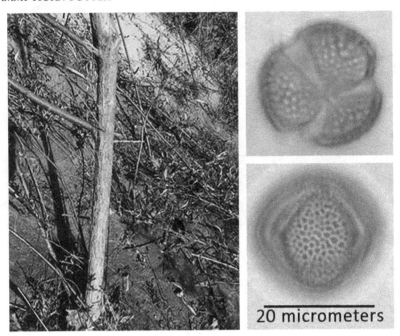

L: Black willow, (*Salix nigra*), young black willow bark and trunk. J. Perry. 2019. UR: *Salix* pollen, polar view, courtesy of J. O'Keefe, 2019. LR: *Salix* pollen, equatorial view, courtesy of J. O'Keefe, 2019.

In terms of uses, willows "clean up" areas, leeching out dioxins and heavy metals in contaminated soils[55]. According to Colin Tudge, willow is an important "fuel wood, now vaunted as a source of biomass to supply energy without contributing to global warming."[56] Willows often provide erosion control because of their strong root systems and rapid upward growth. However, in other places, willows are considered weeds and even almost invasive.[57]

There is a price that this pioneer species will pay for its muscular advancement of a forest line, says Wohlleben. As the willows grow, they provide shade for the slower-growing species. "The pioneer species have no choice but to shade [the slower-growing maples], and when they do, they are signing their own death warrants."[58] Willows have to give way to slower-growing competition. Yet, their strategy to disperse their pollen was achieved by being the first to deliver nectar to winter clusters of honey bees and so beekeepers would be wise to recognize the value of this pioneer species and plant several if they have the space.

The United States would do well to emulate the food standards adopted by the European Union.
[55] Richard Powers' *Overstory*.
[56] Tudge, *The Tree*, 175.
[57] For more information, check out www.willowpedia.com
[58] Wohlleben, 184.

Pussy willow (*Salix discolor*) catkin, a bright yellow that shows up in early spring, attracting pollinators. L. Connor.

MAPLES (ACER SPP.)

Whereas willows take advantage of wide open spaces to populate an area, maples tend to be slower and "more social" in the tree community, to quote Peter Wohlleben. In contrast to a willow, which produces a padded seed that can be blown far away from its source, a maple tree produces heavier seed, thereby ensuring that its seed fall closer the drip line of its source where moisture is more likely, and the seed will not dry in the sun. "The maples are recognized for their fruits, which are paired keys, which spin helicopter-style in the wind and elegantly known in botanical circles as 'samaras.'"[59] With over 150 species of maple in North America, many beehives respond favorably to the pollen and nectar these maples provide in early spring when there are few other nutrition sources. Red maples (*Acer rubrum*) start blooming in February and can last several weeks. On days that reach above 55°F, when honey bees begin to emerge from the hive, a beekeeper can see beeswax cells filled with red pollen from these trees. Sugar maple (*A. saccarum*) and silver maple (*A. saccharinum*) are common in the Central Appalachian region. Beekeeper author and scientist Diana Sammataro reports that in the Northeastern states, the Norway maple (*Acer platanoides*) is also a good species for honey bees, with honey being a pale amber.[60] While this may true in that region, biologist Shannon Trimboli cautions that in some states (Illinois, Indiana, Pennsylvania, Virginia, and West Virginia), the Norway maple is now considered an invasive.[61] Describing how honey bees and other insects respond to maple trees in bloom, Lovell mentions that "their contented hum is audible at a long

[59]Tudge, *The Tree*, 224.
[60]Diana Sammataro and Ann Harman, *Major Flowers Important to Honey Bees in the Northeast and mid-Atlantic States,* 2nd edition. Tucson, AZ: AlphaGraphics, 2013.
[61]Trimboli, 47.

L: Red maple (*Acer rubrum*) flowers. M. Connor. 2019.
R: Red maple (*Acer rubrum*) seeds form samaras, light weight seeds that the wind picks up and disperses easily in the spring. My deck was covered with hundreds. 2019.

distance." Still, according to Lovell, "Maples bloom so early in the season that their value as honey plants is usually greatly underestimated."[62]

In Appalachia, red maples are considered by the Office of Surface Mining a "high value" hardwood, so it is planted with routine frequency as part of rec-lamation. Colin Tudge mentions that maples support an enormous biomass of insects, which in the great chain of life, also supports birds. In describing the sugar maple, Tudge wryly notes that "of the many routes to obesity on offer in the United States, that of crisp bacon, a stack of buckwheat pancakes, and maple syrup is the most seductive of all."[62.1]

In Kentucky, bee brood "buildup" begins in earnest when maple species bloom. Some beekeepers, counting on the maple pollen, will "reverse" their hives around Valentine's Day, weather permitting. This process of reversal is simply placing the bottom box (often called a "brood box" in beekeeper-par-lance), which should be empty of honey bees, on the top, where the honey "super" is. This method of "reversal" allows the winter cluster room to move up and out as the days get longer. As the weather warms, the beekeeper can either make a split by removing the top super and taking to another yard, or simply "reverse" again before the nectar flow starts and makes boxes heavy.

Red maples earn fans in the fall for their spectacular scarlet foliage. It is defi-nitely a high-value tree in more ways than one!

[62]Lovell,155.
[62.1] Trudge, The Tree, 224.

20 micrometers

Captions for page 51.
U: Red pollen being used in bee bread by the honey bees.
M: Tree crown. J. Perry. 2019.
LL: Trunk of a mature tree. J. Perry. 2019.
LM: Red maple (*Acer rubrum*) pollen grain, polar view. J. O'Keefe. 2019.
LR: Equatorial view. J. O'Keefe. 2019.

THE UNDERSTORY

Once the maple trees bloom, the Appalachian understory trees explode in a full flush of redbuds, dogwoods, serviceberry, pawpaw, and persimmon trees. As far as the timber industry was concerned for much of the twentieth century, understory species were "trash trees" because they generated little market value in terms of lumber, furniture production, railroad ties, telephone poles, cabinetry and the other myriad ways that trees contribute to civilization. However, as I watch the understory trees bloom in the spring, they remind me of ballerinas warming up before their performances, the type that Edward Degas would capture in his impressionistic paintings. Just like the dancers, these trees provide a service to humanity, more than mere decorative "landscape trees. The unsung trees provide a "safety net" for bees, providing nutrition if February and March ice and snowstorms render the willow and maples useless.

REDBUD TREES (CERCIS CANADENSIS)

Eastern redbud (*Cercis canadensis*) blossoms. 2019.

Eastern redbud (*Cercis canadensis*) an understory tree. 2019.

Flowering dogwood (*Cornus florida*), and Eastern redbud (*Cercis canadensis*) along a country lane. J. Perry. 2019.

L: Eastern redbud (*Cercis canadensis*) seeds. 2019. R: Bark of Eastern redbud. 2019.

A native understory used in hedges and decorative landscapes, Eastern redbud trees are the "ballerinas" of the understory trees with profuse pink blossoms emerging from twigs and branches. Even the trunks will have pink blossoms, a trait more commonly associated with tropical trees. These trees typically are pollinated by long-tongued bees such as carpenter bees *(Xylocopa virginica)*. Short-tongued bees apparently cannot reach the nectaries, but both Lovell and Diana Sammataro agree that its pollen is important to brood-rearing for honey bees.

The "cercis" is Greek for "weaver's shuttle," and refers to the fruit of this tree, which resembles a shuttle by mid-summer, when the flowers are replaced by bean-like seed pods (legumes).[63] In some parts of southern Appalachia, green twigs from the eastern redbud are used as seasoning for wild game such as venison and opossum. Because of this, in these mountain areas the eastern redbud is sometimes known as the spicewood tree. Biologist Shannon Trimboli mentions that the blossoms have a "peppery punch" when added to salads, enough of an occurrence that another common name for this tree is "salad tree."[64]

The Eastern redbud figures prominently in Appalachia Christian narrative and is known as the Judas tree. When one of the disciples named Judas, who identified Christ to Roman authorities, felt such shame about his betrayal, he decided to use a redbud to hang himself. The tree, in response, blushed at the prospect of being used in this way and vowed to never be strong enough for such purpose again. The redbud wood is brittle, its flowers a showy pink, and when the blossoms fall, wide heart-shaped leaves appear. This species is so similar to a species in Judea, *Cercis siliquastrum*, that some suspect that "Judea" eventually merged into "Judas." In the fall, the heart-shaped leaves of this tree turn a lovely sunny yellow.

DOGWOODS (CORNUS SPP.)

Dogwoods bloom in synchronicity with the Eastern redbuds in Kentucky in April so the two often appear together, forming lines of floral "ballerinas." The flowering dogwood (*Cornus florida*) is distinctive for its flat-topped flowers (called bracts), its lateral limbs, and its small but striking profile in the spring landscapes, whether in a forest surrounded by tall timber or in a suburb in highly-manicured lawns. Donald Wyman, a horticulturist stated, "There is a dogwood for almost every part of the U.S. except the hottest and driest areas. Colin Tudge remarks that there are over 45 species.[65]

[63]"Eastern Redbud, Bernheim Arboretum. https://bernheim.org/learn/trees-plants/bernheim-select-ur-ban-trees/eastern-redbud/
[64]Trimboli, 52.
[65]Colin Tudge, *The Tree: A Natural History of What Trees Are, How They Live, and Why They Matter*, New York: Random House, 2005. 227.

Carpenter bee (*Xylocopa virginica*),
courtesy of
https://ohioline.osu.edu/factsheet/ent-85

U: Flowering dogwood (*Cornus florida*),
understory. 2019.
L: Flowering dogwood (*Cornus florida*),
bracts. 2019.

When other plants are pruned to be perfectly straight, the stocky tree stands out for its distinctive four-part petal structure of its flowers. These flowers are host plants for some butterfly species, and as the flowers become berries, birds are attracted to the fruit. The leaves turn a deep-soft red color in the fall, making dogwoods a landscape staple. According to Lovell, in 1926, he mentions that Divide, West Virginia, the hillsides were covered with dogwoods visited by honey bees.[66]

Among beekeepers, dogwoods are not seen as highly beneficial for honey bees. However, since I have my honey analyzed on an annual basis, I can see that honey bees bring dogwood pollen to their hives when winter extends into February and early March. As already mentioned, the early spring pollens typically are maples and willows. However in 2015, that pattern showed a remarkable change: dogwood was the primary spring pollen. This would be because on February 15, 2015, a foot of snow blanketed Central Appalachia. Another round of snow followed the first week of March. I have not seen dogwood pollen since, but the point is that a variety of flowering species is beneficial to pollinators. The beekeeper cannot possibly predict the weather patterns, so planting various species can provide nutrition when other sources are impacted by weather.

The wood of the dogwood tree is very durable since it has almost no heartwood. One person theorized

[66]John Lovell, *Honey Plants of North America*, A.I. Root, Medina Ohio, 1926, 122.

that "dogwood" is actually a version of Old English "dagwood," since daggers, arrows and knives needed a durable wood for handles. In this region, dogwood was also used to make walking canes, dulcimers, and other tools necessary for either farms and/or household tasks. Similar to the Eastern redbud, an Appalachian Christian narrative features the dogwood as the timber used to build a cross to carry Christ. The legend goes that the dogwood tree had once been straight until the tree was harvested to make crosses. Feeling humiliated at being used for this mission, the dogwood tree expressed its shame. Its punishment was to remain dwarfed in the landscape, but its showy flowers compensate for its stature. Other uses for dogwood suggest that small parts for wagons were made from it because the durable wood could withstand travel and weather.

Rough-leaf dogwood (*Cornus drummondii*) leaves and flowers. The author is grateful to Janine Baker for use of her garden for these photos. 2019.

Although the flowering dogwood (*Cornus florida*) tends to be the most popular of the dogwoods, a lesser-known variety that is native to Kentucky, the rough-leaf dogwood (*Cornus drummondii*), will actually extend the nectar season a bit longer as it blooms from May to July. Since the rough-leaf dogwood is a quickly-growing species, ecologists recommend this variety in the fight against an invasive plant known as bush honeysuckle (*Lonicera morrowii* and *Lonicera maackii*). The rough-leaf dogwood can outcompete bush honeysuckle, and it volunteers itself very easily in disturbed soil and is used for erosion control as well as providing nutrition to butterflies and bees. Its distinctive leaf is aptly-named, feeling like soft sandpaper. Biologist Shannon Trimboli first brought my attention to this species. "The flowers are highly attractive to many different pollinators including honey bees, native bees, butterflies, and many others," writes Trimboli. "In late summer and early fall, the pollinated flowers will form clusters of white fruit. Songbirds and other wildlife will eagerly devour the fruit."

L: Rough-leaf dogwood (*Cornus drummondii*) bark. 2019. R: Rough-leaf dogwood (*Cornus drummondii*), full tree. The author is grateful to Janine Baker for use of her garden for both these photos. 2019.

SERVICEBERRY TREE (AMELANCHIER SPP.)

Bee botanist Connie Krochmal gushes that serviceberry "is a source of beauty, the year around." The plants are best known for their masses of small, delicate, star-like blossoms that cover the plants. Appearing in long clusters at the ends of the shoots, these emerge as the leaves unfurl."[67] The serviceberry tree blooms around Easter; hence, it is often called "sarvis" in the Appalachian region, some say that the spelling is a close approximation of the Appalachian accent pronouncing "service." This shrub tends to bloom when temperatures are warm. People associate its bloom time with a season when it is more feasible for people to attend church or civil services. It is so prevalent across the country that it is also known as shadtree, "for it blooms when the shad run." Shad is a type of "bait" fish upon which bass often fed.

When the serviceberry blooms, the unisexual or bisexual blooms contain five narrow petals and a green, bell-like, five-lobed calyx," according to Krochmal. "A cluster can contain a dozen or more flowers. Usually tasty and edible, the showy, seedy fruits, which are enjoyed by birds, vary in color and shape by species. Forming clusters, these are quick to ripen in Summer. Round to pear-shaped, the berries can be red, almost black, purple, purplish-black, or blue-black. About the size of a blueberry, the fruits were an important food for Native Americans and pioneers."

---

[67]Connie Krochmal, "Native Serviceberries," *Bee Culture*, Feb. 22, 2016. https://www.beeculture.com/native-serviceberries/

L: Serviceberry (*Amelanchier* spp.), blossoms, J. Perry, 2019. R: Serviceberry (*Amelanchier* spp.), full tree. The author is grateful to Janine Baker for use of her garden for these photos. 2019.

Honey bee hives in Eastern Kentucky benefit from serviceberry. A professor at Morehead State University, Dr. Jen O'Keefe has found pollen grains from this tree in many of the honey samples that she and her students process at Morehead State University.

There are 23 species of serviceberry in North America, and it furnishes both pollen and nectar. It does well in urban and suburban areas too, so it is something that vegetation managers may want to consider. Always calling attention to a tree species' bark, botanist Krochmal mentions, "The furrowed, scaly, light gray to silver bark lends color to the landscape during the Winter months." Then it blooms in the mid-spring, providing an explosion of white color, and finally, its foliage in the fall is, in her words, "exquisite."[68]

PawPaw Trees (Asimina Triloba)

"A sheepdog of trees"[69]

"Biggest, best, weirdest, wildest native fruit this continent ever made" is how Richard Powers describes the pawpaw fruit. Resembling a green mango in size and structure, pawpaws can be durable when they have not fully ripened.

[68]Ibid, 66
[69]Richard Powers, *The Overstory*, 115.

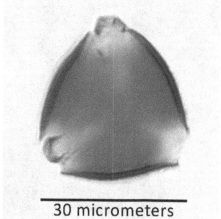

30 micrometers

UL: Serviceberry (*Amelanchier* spp.), leaves
and fruit. L. Connor. 2019.
UR: Serviceberry (*Amelanchier* spp.), pollen,
polar view. V. Bryant. 2019.
LR: Serviceberry (*Amelanchier* spp.), trunk and
bark. J.Perry. 2019.

When my father and uncle were growing up as boys in Harlan County, they would use unripe pawpaws as makeshift weapons to throw at each other. Yet, when the pawpaws are ripe in the fall, typically September in Kentucky, the fruit will fall open to reveal a soft "buttery pulp and shiny black seeds." When Powers' character Patty takes her first bite of a pawpaw, she wants to 'scream with pleasure, but her mouth is full of butterscotch pudding."

The only fruit-bearing tropical tree to survive the Appalachian forest' transition from tropic to the mesic during the Miocene, the pawpaw is a contradiction: it is small understory tree with the largest fruit native to North America. Somehow, this tree species has survived, in no small part because it colonizes a site, sending out suckers forming a "pawpaw patch" from which future generations will develop.

L: Pawpaw (*Asimina triloba*) fruit, Kentucky State University, https://www.facebook.com/ksu.pawpaw/

R: Pawpaw (*Asimina triloba*), pulp and seeds, Kentucky State University, https://www.facebook.com/ksu.pawpaw/

Pawpaws are dioecious, meaning that some trees provide female flowers and others provide male. Both male and female trees need to be in proximity to each other in order for fruit to set. Honey bees will seek the pawpaw pollen when it blooms in April. A botanist for the National Park Service, Elizabeth Matthews writes that pawpaws trees in a cluster are often genetically identical and connected underground by roots (and thus, in biological terms, are a single plant). Nonetheless, pawpaw's pollinators (which include flies and beetles) inevitably pollinate some flowers, and fruit-hunters may eventually find a tree with fruit.[70]

Since surface mine companies cannot plant orchards as part of post-mine reclamation practices, pawpaws have not been included in reforestation; however, given that the pawpaw is native and the Eastern KY region is where this fruit-bearing tree does best, perhaps in the future, this species may be included in some areas.

---

[70]Elizabeth Matthews, "Pawpaw: Small Tree, Big Impact," https://www.nps.gov/articles/pawpaw.htm

PERSIMMON (DIOSPYROS VIRGINIANA)

"Good for dogs, hogs, and 'possums'"

Blooming later in the spring in Appalachia, persimmon trees are dependent on bees for pollination. While the pollen can be carried by wind, it also needs to have pollinators because persimmon trees are dioecious: some trees have male blossoms and some trees host female blossoms.[71]

According to Lovell, persimmon used to be a good resource for early spring buildup because it used to be more widely spread throughout the southeast, such as the Carolinas and Virginia. It does stretch as far west as Kansas. According to Shannon Trimboli, "Persimmons are an important source of food for wildlife. The fruit can also be collected for puddings, breads, and sweets."[72] The native persimmon yields a yellow sapwood that can be used for tool handles. "Textile shuttles made from it are said to last one thousand hours before they wear out," says Tudge.[73]

Bee Culture botanist Connie Krochmal recommends persimmon trees for bee gardens, rattling off a number of distinctive attributes: its deeply furrowed bark looks like "alligator hide," its longevity (it can reach the "century mark,") it can tolerate a wide variety of soils, including surface mine sites, but also urban environments.

---

[71]Lovell, 187.
[72]Trimboli, 89.
[73]Tudge *The Tree*, 230.

L: Pawpaw (*Asimina triloba*). Mature tree with suckers forming a patch. The author is grateful to Janine Baker for use of her garden for these photos. 2019. R: Pawpaw (*Asimina triloba*) blossom. M. Connor. 2019.

UL: Possum in a persimmon tree (*Diospyrios virginiana*), NCSU. L. Bradley. https://gardening. ces.ncsu.edu/2015/12/look-who-came-to-breakfast/
UR: Persimmon blossom (*Diospyros virginiana*). Wikipedia photo. https://en.wikipedia.org/ wiki/Diospyros_virginiana
MR: Fruit of persimmon tree (*Diospyrios virginiana*). Virginia Native Plant Society. September 28, 2017. https://www.facebook.com/VirginiaNativePlantSociety/posts/shake-them-simmons-down-fruit-of-the-native-tree-diospyros-virginiana-is-beginni/1656767341021067/
LL: Persimmon bark (*Diospyrios virginiana*). Wikipedia photo. https://en.wikipedia.org/wiki/

Always promoting a unique aspect of a tree's beauty, Krochmal notes that depending on the species, the persimmon trees can turn purple, yellow or red in the Fall.[74] Krochmal mentions that depending on the species, bees will work

[74]Krochmal, "Persimmons for the Garden," *Bee Culture*, Oct. 15, 2015. https://www.beeculture.com/persimmons-for-the-garden/

persimmon blossoms from sunrise to sunset. The flower structure prevents the nectar from washing away during the rain. Although she says all varieties of persimmons are easy to grow, she does recommend starting with a ball-and-burlap as persimmons are slow growers and do not like to be transplanted.

Readers, take note: do not eat the fruit of a persimmon before it is ripe! Krochmal describes the fruit as, "astringent," but even that is too mild an adjective. However, it is delicious once ripe. Of all the varieties, Krochmal recommends the American persimmon variety because its "smooth-skinned fruits are richer flavored and smaller than those from Asian trees. Variable in shape, they're typically plum or tomato-shaped with deep orange to yellow skins blushed with red."

To discern if the fruit is ripe, the fruit should feel mushy. Then, and only then, should one attempt to eat it, although Krochmal says that frost is not necessary to make it edible. It is a major nectar source in at least five states (Krochmal mentions Virginia, Missouri, Arkansas, Oklahoma, and Kansas by name) and of some value in 22 other states. Both nectar and pollen are available, and the honey derived from persimmon is light to amber.

BLACK LOCUSTS (ROBINIA PSEUDOACACIA)

"Stones will crumble before locusts will rot"[75]

Beginning in late April or early May, black locust trees with their bountiful grape-like blossoms (called *racemes*) will dominate the fence rows on my farm, on highway rights-of-ways, and the edges of surface mine sites. Most of the years that coal companies held Arbor Day events, black locusts were included in the mix, although there were one or two years that seedlings were difficult to obtain. The advantages for the coal companies is that black locusts, being in the legume family, grow quickly and fix nitrogen to soils. For executives wanting their bond money returned from the federal government (some of which were millions of dollars), substantial stands of black locusts could indicate successful reclamation efforts.

For beekeepers, black locusts almost drip with flowers bearing nectar. So stunning is this display that the black locust is said to be responsible for the environmentalist John Muir's life-long quest of conservation. When he was a student at the University of Wisconsin, a fellow student handed Muir a raceme from a black locust and asked him to identify the family of the tree. Muir thought for a second, "It is like a pea flower." Muir was correct, but confused. "How can that be when the pea is a weak, clinging, straggling herb, and the locust a big thorny hardwood tree?" When he realized that both a pea

[75]Lovell, 149

and a black locust belonged to the same family, he began a lifetime journey into botanical studies. Muir writes, "This fine lesson charmed me and sent me flying to the woods and meadows in wild enthusiasm. Like everyone else, I was always fond of flowers, attracted by their external beauty and purity. Now my eyes were opened to their inner beauty, all alike revealing glorious traces of the thoughts of God, and leading on and on into the infinite cosmos."[76]

Although black locusts are native to Appalachia, they are considered an invasive in some states because they reproduce (asexually) by sending out root suckers in addition to being pollinated by insects. Since bush honeysuckle has been introduced in the Bluegrass, the black locusts on my farm are welcome, for these trees can outcompete the invasive honeysuckle.

As with willows, which has been considered a source for biofuel in New York and West Virginia research experiments, black locust timber is distinctive for its high British Thermal Unit count (28 million BTU per cord), a measure of how much heat is produced when burning.[77] Compared to coal, which emits sulfur dioxide as it burns and hence earns the moniker "dirty coal," black locust can produce a clean-burning heat, replacing, theoretically, coal in

---

[76]John Muir, *The Story of My Boyhood and Youth* (Boston & New York: Houghton Mifflin, 1913), 280-83.
[77]Willow measures measuring 14 million British Thermal Units per cord wood, which is not as high as black locust, but given the other advantages of willow, may be one more use for it as a timber crop. For more information about this effort, go to www.willowpedia.com.

Black locust (*Robinia pseudoacacia*) flowers, branch and leaves. 2019.

UL: Black locust, (l) several trees in a row, 2019. UR: Black Locust, (*Robinia pseudoacacia*) racemes. 2019. ML: Black locust (*Robinia pseudoacacia*) pollen grain, polar view. J. O'Keefe. 2019. LL: equatorial view. J. O'Keefe. 2019. LR: Black locust (*Robinia pseudoacacia*) bark. J. Perry. 2019.

some cases. At one point in 2009, a coal company executive named Richard Addington had considered planting "black locust plantations," which meant large acreages of black locusts allowed to grow for three years. At the three year-mark, the black locusts would be cut to prompt the trees to send out new suckers. In fact, there is record of large plantations being planted for timber in John Lovell's *Honey Plants of North America*.[78] When this idea was being considered, suckers would be allowed to grow to "market value" to harvest, but in the meantime, the bees could benefit from the fields of black locust blooms. Although Addington's plan for a clean biofuel using black locust never worked out (natural gas has supplanted coal and Addington's company went out of business), black locust trees make good fence posts, so there are multiple markets for this species.

Although it is now considered an invasive in Connecticut, Wisconsin, and Massachusetts, black locust honey, often water-white, fetches top dollar on the honey market.

---

[78]Lovell, 149.

Black locust (*Robinia pseudoacacia*) full tree in blossom. 2019.

UL: Tulip poplar (*Liriodendron tulipifera*), blossom. J. Perry. 2019.
UR: Pollen grain. J. O'Keefe. 2019
ML: Trunk. J. Perry. 2019. MR: crown, J. Perry. 2019.
BL: Full tree. 2019. BR: Leaf and bud. 2019.

Tulip poplar (*Liriodendron tulipifera*), blooms. 2019.

TULIP POPLAR (LIRIODENDRON TULIPIFERA)

The "handsomest of American ornamental trees,"[79]

While it is not a true poplar, belonging instead to the Magnolia family, the tulip poplar bloom looks exactly like a 'tulip," with six large petals surrounding many stamens.[80] While the outside of the petals may be creamy-white and greenish, the inside of the petals are mango-yellow. These serve as both nectaries and nectar guides. In the center of the stamens is a cone-like mass of pistils.

Honey bees and hummingbirds will visit these tulip poplar flowers many times, although it can be an unreliable source for nectar because of frequent rain. The honey made from tulip poplar typically is dark honey, as dark as molasses. According to Lovell, "when the blossoms are late in opening and the weather is warm and dry, the honey is very much heavier than when the tree blooms early….Under such conditions, there are few if any better honey plants than the tulip tree."[81]

It is considered a "high value hardwood" and is almost always included in reforestation efforts on surface mine sites. As the surface mining laws were translated into actions in 1977, coal companies began to consider reforestation with high value hardwoods because by reforesting these areas, companies could help set up a long-term industry (i.e. timber) that could also help reduce erosion and control flooding. Tulip poplar produces lumber needed for homes and cabinetry. It also been used as pulpwood. Given its length and durability, Native Americans used to use tulip poplars for canoes, although I daresay that its purpose for canoes has since passed. Its wood can resist insects if the wood is dry. It is difficult to overestimate how important this tree is to Appalachian beekeepers.

HOLLY (ILEX SPP.)

"Holly hath birds a fair full flock,
The nightingale, the popinjay, the gentle laverock"
Nay, Ivy, nay, it shall not be I wis;
Let holly have the mastery, as the manner is[82]

While holly trees were not included as part of the Appalachian Regional Reforestation Initiative, their importance to the pollinators in this region is undeniable and they grow wild in forest pockets. In the Appalachian region,

---

[79]Lovell, 224.
[80]Sammataro and Harman mention that it is related to the magnolia.
[81]Lovell, 225.
[82]From the English Carol, "The Contest between the Holly and the Ivy," collected by Cecil Sharp

UL: Holly (*Ilex spp.*), blossoms. 2019. UR: Berries. 2018.
LL: Holly (*Ilex spp.*), pollen grain, polar view, J. O'Keefe. 2019. LR: Holly (*Ilex spp.*), pollen grain, equatorial view. J. O'Keefe, 2019.

hollies bloom around the middle of May with an abundance of small white flowers. A holly provides copious amounts of nectar and pollen. In addition, the small red berries provide important sources of nutrition for songbirds. The relationship between hollies and birds is captured in many folks songs, including an English medieval carol, "The Contest of the Ivy and the Holly," in which the holly hosts owls, nightingales, popinjay, and laverock, a veritable "full flock." In Appalachian Christian narratives, the holly is a prominent image, the spiked leaves often serving as the crown of thorns worn by Christ, and red berries symbolizing drops of blood sacrificed for his followers.

More probably, according to Colin Tudge, many hollies have developed thick-skinned leaves and some of these leaves have sharp thorny spikes to prevent being browsed by deer. Hollies tend to be a smaller tree, and so have to spend enormous energy defending themselves. Comparing the hollies to palms that live in tropical forests surrounded by predators and must be "spiked as fiercely as the walls of a medieval prison," Tudge explains that hollies tend to invest their energies in creating spiked leaves on the lower part of the tree trunk to discourage browsing in the upper levels of the tree.[83]

Hollies are dioecious, meaning some trees only produce male flowers, others produce only female flowers. In a well-written article titled "Holly Berry," *Bee Culture* author Paul Snyder instructs gardeners to buy two holly trees if they are considering buying a holly because "in order to get berries, you need a male pollinator." Furthermore, the male and female holly plants must belong to the same species, must be planted somewhat near each other and must bloom at the same time.[84]

For folks interested in native species, the winterberry holly (*Ilex verticillata)* is an impressive choice. It is deciduous and "the stark gray stems are absolutely stunning when covered in red berries," Snyder said. Bluebirds eat the berries, sustaining them through the wintertime. Another native holly species (*Ilex decidua*) that is deciduous is the possumhaw, which also blooms around the same time as the black locust and tulip poplar.

The American holly (*Ilex opaca*) resembles the English holly (*Ilex aquifolium)*, with glossy green leaves and red or yellow berries, so many people substitute it for holiday decorating. However, the American holly is a slow grower, taking decades to reach 40-50 feet. "When you come across a large specimen, there's almost a respect for the plant. It's a noble tree in its own right because it took decades to reach such heights," according to Snyder.

---

[83]Tudge, *The Tree*, 354.
[84]Kurt Knebusch and Paul Snyder, "Holly Bee," *Bee Culture*, Jan. 23, 2017. https://www.beeculture. com/holly-bee/

UL: Wild Cherry, (*Prunus serotina*) mature. 2019. URT: Seeds, leaves, 2019.
M: Blossom. M. Connor. 2019
LL: Wild Cherry, (*Prunus serotina*) pollen, polar, J. O'Keefe
LR: Wild Cherry, (*Prunus serotina*) pollen, equatorial, J. O'Keefe

WILD CHERRY (PRUNUS SPP.)

A pioneer tree, wild cherry trees grow readily throughout the Ohio and Tennessee Valleys and can bloom from March-May, depending on the species. According to Peter Wohlleben, wild cherry blossoms are unusual compared to other trees because both "male and female sex organs are on the same blossom," and "one of the true forest trees that allow themselves to be pollinated by bees. As the bees make their way through the whole crown, they cannot help but spread the tree's own pollen."[85] The wild cherry tree has a test to prevent inbreeding. "When a pollen grain lands on a stigma," explains Wohlleben, "its genes are activated and it grows a delicate tube down to the ovary in search of an egg. As it is doing this, the tree tests the genetic makeup of the pollen, and if it matches its own, blocks the tube, which then dries up."

Wild cherries also produce seeds that can lie dormant for up to five years, waiting for just the right conditions to sprout. This can be advantageous on disturbed soils that may experience drier conditions than an otherwise lush forest environment.

Highly-valued for its wood in cabinetry and furniture, wild black cherry is a large tree with oblong and slender leaves. Depending on soil conditions, Lovell writes that in the Northern states, the pigeon cherry secretes nectar freely, and furthermore, "it blooms after the domestic fruits and just before the opening of white clover, so it should provide of considerable value."[86] Yet, he quotes other beekeepers that suggest it is not a valuable source of honey. Melissopalynologist Jen O'Keefe has pollen from wild cherries, suggesting that in Appalachia, honey bees actively visit wild cherry blossoms and return to the hives with pollen.

BASSWOOD TREE (TILIA AMERICANA)

A "cradle to coffin" tree

To be near a blooming basswood tree is to instinctively want to immerse oneself into the center of its bower and remain there, listening to the song of insects and inhaling the scent of the blossoms luring all the winged insects far and wide. So important is this tree to Appalachia that it is considered a "cradle to coffin" tree, providing the comforts of home in furniture, shelter, and coffin all made from the beautifully blonde basswood.[87] Its broad leaves

---

[5]Wohlleben, 22.

[6]Lovell, 439-440.

[7]The other "cradle to coffin" tree was the American chestnut (Castanea dentate). It was the dominate canopy tree until a blight appeared in North America in the twentieth century. Efforts are now being made to modify the American chestnut, but still needs more research.

Basswood (*Tilia americana*) tree.
Basswood is known as a "cradle to coffin tree in Appalachia. W. Overbeck. 2013.

UL: Basswood (*Tilia americana*), blossoms. 2018.
UR: Basswood (*Tilia americana*), trunk and crown. W. Overbeck. 2013.
LL: Basswood (*Tilia americana*), leaf. 2018.
LR: Basswood (*Tilia americana*), bark and trunk. 2019.

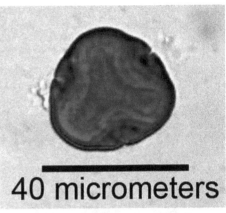

40 micrometers

L: Basswood (*Tilia americana*), leaf, dorsal view. 2019. R: Basswood (*Tilia Americana*), pollen grain. J. O'Keefe. 2019.

protect clusters of flowers from rain, and insects shimmer from blossom to blossom in midsummer heat.

In Appalachia, the basswood tree tends to bloom in the second week of June, providing nectar and pollen at a critical time after the spring-flowering trees have gone out of bloom but before the wildflowers erupt in profusion.[88] Basswood trees have "high value" for lumber and provide a light nectar that becomes, once processed by honey bees, an exquisite light honey varietal. Lovell writes that the nectar is secreted and "it is often so abundant that it appears like dewdrops in the sunlight."[89] Lovell notes that when nectar flow is abundant, rarely do the bees bother trying to collect pollen. However, if there is a slow nectar flow, then both honey bees and bumble bees will gather nectar and pollen.

No surprise that this tree is the symbol of hospitality in Greek mythology. In the myth, Baucis and her husband Philemon are a poor but generous married couple who offer a meager meal and lodging to Zeus and Hermes, two gods dressed as strangers who knock on their door after being turned away by everyone else in the village. When the gods reveals themselves to the older couple, they are angry at the nearby villagers, who refused to help the disguised gods, shutting doors in their faces. They decide to destroy the village, but the gods reward Baucis and Philemon for their kindness by being allowed to die together, transforming into a linden (Baucis) and an oak (Philemon) with intertwined roots.

[88]These massive trees used to be in both forest and suburban environments until the massive snowstorms of the mid-1970s meant cities had to expend much of their budgets on tree removals. Richard Weber, Spring House Gardens, Lexington, Kentucky. Interview July 03, 2014.
[89]Lovell, 69.

The little leaf linden (*Tilia cordata*) is a cousin to the basswood (*Tilia Americana*). It blooms slightly later than the basswood trees, providing both nectar and pollen. Although pollinators seem to work it regardless, Shannon Trimboli thinks the fact that this tree is not as common and/or is in urban or suburban environments, people are not as aware of its importance. Its importance is confined to local and limited areas, not the widespread importance that the basswood has to states and regions.[90.1]

SOURWOOD (OXYDENDRUM ARBORETUM)

The Appalachian Lily of the Valley

Appalachian sourwood honey defies easy description, but elicits hushed respect and cautious respectful inquiries about sources and also geographical locations where one can set one's hives.

Its Greek name, "oxys" means "sour," and refers to the leaves, not the honey, which act as a chemical defense of the smaller-statured tree. The tree itself is distinctive in urban environments because in the autumn, it will turn a brilliant red, providing outstanding color. Even in the summer heat, when it is still green, it sends out its flowers like fireworks, providing nectar around the middle of June through the Fourth of July.

Local folks call it "the Appalachian Lily of the Valley." Its flowers, called pendulums, are curved to resemble a floral bell pointing downward. This structure prevents rain from washing nectar away. Yet, even though the flowers are working in the favor of beekeepers, not every year will result in a sourwood nectar flow. In my experience, about one in four years, my hives had substantial enough sourwood nectar to produce some honey.

Compounding the difficulty of marketing a true sourwood varietal, the tree does not produce much sourwood pollen. Compared to other flowers, sourwood may only produce a grain or two of pollen per flower. Aggravating the issue is that even if a honey bee picks up a grain of pollen, the grain may fall

[90.1]In a personal communication to the author, Dr. Jen O'Keefe extrapolates on the difficulties of relying on pollen to determine a monofloral varietal: We've known for a long time that 45% was not a great number. Molan in 1998 pointed this out rather succinctly (https://www.umf.org.nz/wp-content/myimages/2017/02/Molan-1998-Pollen-in-honey.pdf). As late as 2017, 45% was still the internationally accepted number (https://onlinelibrary.wiley.com/doi/full/10.1111/1541-4337.12278), but with caveats. By 2018, this had become >20% for unifloral honeys that are from plants with typically "underrepresented" pollen, >45% for those with typically represented pollen, and >70% for those with "overrepresented" pollen in New Zealand...but even that is a moving target. The IBC used Louveaux et al. 1971 and 1978 to make the definition until very recently (2017 or 2018, I think). Now individual countries are defining the pollen content for unifloral honeys, recognizing that 45% may be unobtainable: https://onlinelibrary.wiley.com/doi/full/10.1111/1541-4337.12278. In a way, it is pretty messy right now. We're hampered in the US by not having the huge databases available in other countries. Vaughn can do detailed comparisons among the samples he's analyzed, but Irina and I don't have as many datapoints to compare to, and none of us have the physicochemical data that is routinely available in labs in other countries.

UL: Sourwood, (*Oxydendrum arboretum*), young sourwood tree in full bloom, 2007
UR: blossoms and leaf. 2012.
LL: Sourwood (*Oxydendrum arboretum*), bark. J. Perry. 2019.
LR: Sourwood (*Oxydendrum arboretum*), pollen grain. V. Bryant. 2019.

UL: Sourwood (*Oxydendrum arboretum*), winter crown. J. Perry. 2019.
UR: Mature tree in summer. 2012.
LL: Fall color. 2012.

off the honey bee by the time the bee returns to the hive. Much pollen will fall off the bee in transit. Beekeepers who label their honey as "sourwood" need to have a pollen analysis showing that the percentage of sourwood is at least 45% of sourwood.[90.2]

While timber industry specialists referred to the sourwood as a "trash" tree because it does not have any timber value, beekeepers can make good money from sourwood varietal honey. In 2017, for example, the Savannah Honey Company was selling sourwood honey for $100.00 an ounce. However, sourwood does not produce a nectar flow every single year. It also does not do well as a bare-root seedling: it does not like to be transplanted. Hand-collected seed is a good way to help this species start. It prefers acidic rocky soils in mountainous regions. If someone chooses to purchase a ball-and-burlap sourwood, he or she should make sure that the plant is at least five years old. Of all the varieties that Coal Country Beeworks tried to establish, sourwood was the most difficult. Bare root seedlings are simply not available. When sourwoods did grow, deer browsed them down. I finally began collecting seed by hand on mine sites and simply sowed them. My experience taught me a lesson: reforestation plans should not be a "one-size fits all" template. I have learned to be flexible and promote a species in a way that works to the advantage for both the trees and the company at minimal cost and greater survivability.

I would be remiss if I did not mention that many urban planners make good use of sourwood as a decorative tree. The fall color is spectacular, and in terms of height, the tree will rarely grow over 80 feet in suburban areas. Since this tree grows slowly, it is rather easy to prune and control.

WITCH HAZEL, (HAMAMELIS VIRGINIANA)

aka, winterbloom

Barely visible on the fringes of the forests through the course of the year, the native witch hazel *Hamamelis virginiana* produces pollens in November. For that reason alone, beekeepers should embrace it. As a small tree, it fits in easily with most landscapes. Yet, I suspect that this plant is saddled with baggage of misused or outdated lexicon. The term "witch" does it no favors in this

L: Witch hazel, (*Hamamelis virginiana*), "Winter bloom." 2018.
R: Full tree in autumn. The author is grateful to Kate Black for use of her garden for these photos. 2018.

UL: Witch hazel (*Hamamelis virginiana*), green leaves. 2019. UR: Full tree in spring. 2019.
LL: Winter branch. 2018.
The author is grateful to Kate Black for use of her garden for these photos.

current climate of political correctness. The word "witch" is a hold-over from Middle English "wiche" or Old English, "wice," meaning *pliant* and *bendable* and may be one reason why it can hold its fruit until fall.

Its yellow blossoms in late autumn are an advantage because there is very little competition from other flowering species. It produces nectar to attract pollinators, although only one percent of the flowers ever produce fruit. This is ironic because *hamamelis,* means "together with fruit." According to botanist Amy Aldenderfer, the "seed capsules explode apart with a cracking pop and catapult seeds up to ten yards," thus another alternative name, "Snapping Hazel."[90.2] I must confess: I have not witnessed this event firsthand. Trimboli cautions that exotic versions of witch hazel are more common that the native version, and these exotics have a different bloom schedule (typically February).

In conclusion, reforestation on surface mine sites represents many opportunities for beekeepers. The pollen and nectar-producing trees discussed in this chapter not only provide nutrition and shelter to a diverse array of birds and insects, they can be readily adapted for other landscapes, such as backyards, gardens, and large-scale areas. Other "small tree" species such as sumac volunteer easily on disturbed sites too, and pollen analysis consistently indicate that sumac is a valuable source of nutrition for honey bees. In some areas, corporations such as distilleries, which depend on white oak to age their bourbons, contribute 20,000 seedlings to reforestation events each spring. Most people seem to be able to unify to reduce forest fragmentation, even if in other spheres, they find themselves in polarized environments.

Even though the numbers of trees planted since 2009 can be difficult to quantify (estimates range from 400,000 to several million seedlings), there are nearly one million acres of "legacy mine" acres to reforest in Appalachia as of 2019. By all indications, multiple stakeholders (within the state and region) are aligning to work on those legacy mine sites to make them more productive by planting than they have been in the past. Perhaps by 2029, the legacy sites will be merely a distant memory.

[90.2]Amy Aldenderfer, "Winter is for Witch Hazel," University of Kentucky *Horticulture Newsletter,* 2015, www.uky.edu/hort/.

Chapter Four: The Forbs

When the majority of Appalachian trees cease blooming by June, wildflowers become the primary source for hive nutrition. While I was establishing honey bees on mine sites, a wildlife biologist named Jacob Stewart was increasing wildflower diversity on some of the same surface mine sites. His research, which substituted partridge pea for clovers, meant that other wildflowers could establish their root systems without having to compete with clovers. Of their own violation, the coal company executives provided space for wild-flower plots so that the hives would have access to a diverse three-season bloom. Furthermore, now that I am working with the Kentucky Department of Agriculture, the substitution of partridge pea for clover has worked well with other large-scale vegetation management projects, such as those with the Kentucky Transportation Cabinet and Columbia Gas right-of-ways. The Kentucky Department of Agriculture Pollinator Protection Plan has been a multi-stakeholder effort to increase communication among entities who want to reduce hive mortality, reduce chemical use, and most importantly as far as the public is concerned, increase pollinator habitat. The visibility of pollina-tor habitat zones, whether on a surface mine site or a highway right-of-way or a pipeline, bids well among the public.

It is beyond the scope of this book to provide a definitive list of all the wild-flowers that are good for bees, but this chapter highlights wildflowers that are being planted across the Commonwealth: partridge pea *Chamaecrista fasciculata)*, coreopsis (*Coreopsis lanceolate* and *Coreopsis tinctoria*), purple coneflower *(Echinacea purpurea)*, goldenrod *(Solidago canadensis)*, sun-flower (*Helianthus maximiliani*), and New England aster (*Symphyotrichum novae-angliae*). Blackberries volunteer themselves, and while not part of an established wildflower seed mix, the pollens show up in significant quantities on a consistent basis.

Partridge pea (Chamaecrista fasciculata)

Also known as "sensitive pea"[91]

In 2009, Kentucky experienced a drought of epic proportions. Since I had many first-year hives, I was taking supplemental feed to my apiaries and co-incidentally, saw met up with Jacob Stewart (Kentucky Department of Fish

---

[91]Lovell, 184.

U: Partridge pea, (*Chamaecrista fasciculata*). 2011.
L: Partridge pea (*Chamaecrista fasciculata*) stem and nectary. T.C. Davis. 2014.

and Wildlife). In his experimental plots, clovers (*Melilotus officinalis* and *Melilotus alba*) had been replaced by partridge pea. The plots with partridge pea not only were greener and handling the 2009 drought better, but the other wildflowers were compatible with partridge pea. In contrast, the wildflower plots with clovers were not doing well, especially given the scarcity of water. Clovers were out-competing the other flowers.

Partridge pea is native, does well on a variety of difficult soils, does not outcompete other wildflower varieties, and honey bees could still bring in pollen and nectar. It is no surprise that partridge pea is at the center of national conversations about forage. Some organizations are making strong appeals that all clovers be removed from federal conservation mixes so that native bees can replenish their numbers. Underlying the appeal is the assumption that managed bees such as honey bee hives outcompete native bees when clovers are available. I understand the current dilemma of commercial beekeepers distraught at this suggestion that clovers be removed from federal USDA Conservation Research Project mixes. In managed environments, the clovers are wonderful for honey bees. But in terms of large-scale ground cover, partridge pea does quite well—and more importantly, other forbs do well too.

As a plant, the partridge pea is unusual for its extrafloral nectaries that are on the stem of the plant. This is where honey bees will collect nectar, not the flower itself (Lovell says the flowers are "wholly nectarless"). Partridge pea blooms for a long time during the summer. Lovell adds that nectar can be gathered "continuously for 100 days or more."[92] For all its benefits of providing nectar, Lovell did not much recommend it, saying it has poor flavor. Yet, "inferior as is the flavor of the honey, its fine appearance has caused it to sell at a high price." Remember, Lovell was writing in 1926. For Lovell, the high quantity and long nectar flow "atoned" for the poor quality of honey.

I agree with Lovell: Since droughts are becoming more frequent, I recommend people consider adding partridge pea to their conservation plots. Not necessarily because I like poor quality of honey, but because honey bees do better with a "diversity" of nectars. Partridge pea does not outcompete other wildflowers. For me, this is the most important consideration if I am going to invest in converting farm acreage to pollinator habitat. Since it costs approximately $1,000.00 an acre to convert farmland to pollinator habitat, I want to get the most for the money.

COREOPSIS (COREOPSIS SPP.)

While 2018 marked the Year of the Coreopsis, we would be silly not to celebrate this species every single year. Coreopsis flowers are cheerfully yel-

---

[92] Lovell, 186.

L: Lanceleaf coreopsis flower (*Coreopsis lancelota*), S. Brundage, https://www.wildflower.org/plants/ R: Plains coreopsis (*Coreopsis tinctoria*). J. Marcus. https://www.wildflower.org/plants/

low heralds of summer. The garden writer Norman Winter describes them as "fiery yellow gold." They grow in small areas, but quickly form extensive colonies. Two varieties do well on surface mine sites: the lanceleaf coreopsis (*Coreopsis lancelota)* and the plains coreopsis (*Coreopsis tinctoria*)**.** In fact, to emphasize how well this species can handle drought, Norman Winter says that coreopsis is "tough enough to be planted at your streetside. This is one of the best perennials for the beginner gardener."[93] These species attract many native pollinators, not just honey bees. Song birds will benefit from the seeds in the fall. In my own suburban yard, the species known as threadleaf coreopsis (*Coreopsis verticillata*) does exceptionally well the entire summer.

However, as far as honey production, Shannon Trimboli cautions that this flower may have local importance as a "honey plant, but it [is] not considered a major honey plant" in the region.[94] Depending on the species, coreopsis will bloom the first week of June, which fills a "gap" between the end of the tulip poplar bloom and before the basswood bloom.

PURPLE CONEFLOWER (ECHINACEA PURPUREA)

This stalwart perennial blooms in mid-June and stays blooming throughout the fall into late October. Many pollinators visit this species: The flowers are cross-pollinated by long-tongued bees, bee flies, Halictid bees, skippers, bumble bees, miner bees (*Melissodes* spp.), and leaf-cutting bees (*Megachile* spp.). Butterfly visitors include monarchs, fritillaries, painted ladies, swallowtails, sulfurs, and whites. The caterpillars of the butterfly silvery checker-

---

[93]Norman Winter, "Coreopsis add light in gardens," *Lexington Herald Leader*, May 12, 2019, 4D.
[94]Trimboli, 112.

L: Purple coneflower, (*Echinacea purpurea*). 2016.
R: Plant. 2019.

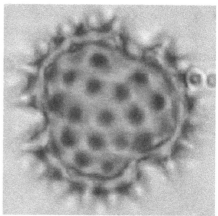
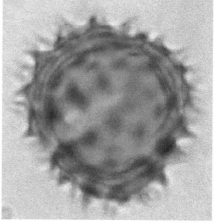

UL: Purple coneflower, (*Echinacea pur-
purea*), seeds. 2019.
UR: Pollen, polar. J. O'Keefe. 2019.
R: Pollen, equatorial. J. O'Keefe. 2019.

U and L: Goldenrod (*Solidago canadensis*). 2012.

spot (*Chlosyne nycteis*) feed on the foliage, while the caterpillars of several moths feed on the flowerheads. If one leaves the seedheads on the stalks during the winter, songbirds such the Eastern Goldfinch will eat the ripe seeds during the summer and early fall. Because this flower is native, perennial, and easy to transplant, it is a great species to introduce into gardens. While this is not a great nectar crop for honey bees, its attractiveness to a wide diversity of pollinators reminds landowners and homeowners that when it comes to honey bees, "it's not all about honey production." Bumble bees will collect pollen from this flower as late as 6:00 p.m. and honey bees will be on it first thing the next morning.

GOLDENROD (SOLIDAGO SPP.)

This bountiful wildflower blooms during the last week of July in Kentucky and stays in bloom until October. There are over 30 varieties in Kentucky alone, and many more throughout the United States. These flowers provide abundant nectar and pollen. Lovell describes the flowers in this way: "although the individual heads are so small, conspicuousness is gained by massing them in great plumelike clusters or panicles."[95] He attributes its popularity with insects to its short floral tube, which allows easy access to most insects. The stately structure of its flowers also can provide temporary refuge for insects that get caught in the rain. He cites S. Graenicher's floral pollinator interactions, with as many 182 insects on the early goldenrod (*Solidago juncea*) and 144 visitors to Canada goldenrod (*Solidago canadensis*), the species planted on the Kentucky surface mine sites. As a sidenote, Lovell offers, four or five of the native wild bees (he did not specify) "fly only in autumn, never visit any other plants."[96]

In general, goldenrod nectar has a unique odor that will eventually dissipate inside the hive, but it is always a strong olfactory cue that hives have been working these flowers. But there are so many species and varying soil conditions impact nectar that one must always take those into consideration. In my experience, Canada goldenrod (*Solidago canadensis*) provides a good, if modest, nectar flow, enough for the hives to make it through winter without supplemental feeding. The one exception was the drought year of 2009, after I had just started some new hives.

Because there are extensive herbarium libraries with goldenrod species, researchers have used goldenrod as a starting point to understand how climate change may impact the quality of pollen. In his article about this research, Dennis O'Brien discusses how Lewis Ziska and his colleagues were thorough in their analysis of how rising carbon dioxide (hereafter, CO_2) levels affect

[95]Lovell, 135.
[96]Lovell, 135.

the pollen of Canada goldenrod (*Solidago canadensis*), the most widespread source of fall protein for honey bees. To study floral demography and insect visitation, researchers counted each goldenrod stem and each insect that visited the stem in Williamstown, Berkshire County, Mass. In the same study but a separate set of research, experimental field trials were conducted in a facility constructed in central Texas to simulate the tallgrass prairie conditions in which goldenrod thrives in the Heartland. Here is a link to the research that offers clarity on the scope of this research: https://royalsocietypublishing.org/doi/full/10.1098/rspb.2016.0414

To get a historical perspective, they analyzed goldenrod pollen from across the United States collected as far back as 1842 and stored at the National Museum of Natural History. Their results showed that the pollen protein levels have declined by up to a third since the 1850s, when atmospheric CO_2 levels began rising, and that the most serious declines have occurred since 1960, when CO_2 levels began rising dramatically. It has been the first study to document the effects of rising CO_2 levels on honey bee diets.[97]

As the Kentucky state flower, goldenrod is ubiquitous in the fall. Goldenrod is used in reclamation projects, highway rights-of-way, and other vegetation projects because the seed is so readily established.

SUNFLOWER (HELIANTHUS SPP.)

A "veritable herbaceous tree"[98]

Native sunflowers are critically important to pollinator nutrition. They provide both pollen and nectar, and for long stretches of time (from June to October, in KY). Lovell cites an example that in Ventura, California (he doesn't give date but presumable before 1926), an entire "carload of sunflower honey" was extracted. I think, but can't be sure, that he means railroad car, but nothing to specify.

Sunflowers also do well on a variety of soils, too. The Maximilian's sunflower (*Helianthus maximiliana*) was used on the Kentucky surface mine sites. Because there are so many species, identification can be difficult, but Maximilian's sunflower has a couple of characteristics: its leaves fold down and it doesn't have as many "teeth" on the edges of the leaves. The nectaries of the sunflowers typically do not produce nectar until the afternoon, so I advise beekeepers to plant buckwheat in the morning to offer something that the bees can work until the sunflowers start producing nectar. Biologist Shannon

[97]Dennis O'Brien, "Changes in Goldenrod: A Key Source of Honey Bee Nutrition, *Catch the Buzz*, June 4, 2016. https://www.beeculture.com/catch-buzz-changes-goldenrod-key-source-honey-bee-nutrition/
[98]Lovell 211.

Sunflowers (*Helianthus maximiliani*) on surface mine sites, 2012.

L: Sunflower (*Helianthus maximiliani*) USDA.
R: Buckwheat (*Fagopyrum esculentum*) planting on a surface mine site near Jenkins, KY. This land was released from bond restrictions, and so the coal company had discretion to plant buckwheat, an annual, on a plot next to the apiary. 2012.

3.25 acres converted to pollinator habitat, Kentucky Transportation Cabinet. 2019.

Trimboli explains that "what we think of as the flower of the sunflower, is actually a composite of many different flowers. The different types of flowers making up the sunflower head serve different roles, much like the different castes of the honey bees in the hive. Only the flowers in the dark center produce seeds."[99]

There has been recent research assessing if sunflowers can counteract the harmful impact of *Nosema ceranae*. Since the antibiotic Fumigilan-B has been taken off the market, beekeepers need a tool to control nosema. Thus far, beekeepers cull old beeswax, presumably, where spores may be stored. Because every year, two million acres in the United States and 10 million acres in Europe are devoted to sunflowers, sunflower pollen is an immediate source of nutrition. The study by researchers at North Carolina State University and the University of Massachusetts Amherst shows two different species of bees fed a diet of sunflower pollen had dramatically lower rates of infection by specific pathogens.[100] "We've tried other monofloral pollens, or pollens coming from one flower, but we seem to have hit the jackpot with sunflower pollen," said Rebecca Irwin, a professor of applied ecology at North Carolina State. Since sunflowers are low in protein and some amino acids, Irwin

[99]Trimboli, 198.
[100]Alan Harman, "Sunflower Pollen Seems to Cause Real Problems for *Nosema ceranae*. That's Good," *Catch the Buzz*, Oct. 18, 2018. https://www.beeculture.com/catch-the-buzz-sunflower-pollen-seems-to-cause-real-problems-for-nosema-ceranae-thats-good/

cautioned against relying on sunflowers as a stand-alone source of pollen. However, it makes a great flower to include with other wildflowers.

ASTER   (SYMPHYOTRICHUM NOVAE-ANGLIAE)

White aster (*Symphyotrichum ericoides*). 2017.

As with goldenrod (*Solidago* spp.), I can typically sense when my honey bees are bringing in New England aster (*Symphyotrichum novae-angliae*), one of many species of aster. The yeasty odor pervades the air when I get out of the truck. The nectar odors will fade. Since my husband and I have already harvested honey for family and friends, the honey produced from this flower's nectar will stay in the hive for the winter clusters.

Asters have a long bloom season, from August until October. Because my farm has two CRP plots (conservation reserve plots), the asters have saved me in terms of "sweat equity": my husband and I typically do not feed our bees. We let the CRP fields provide the nutrition because, in the words of Lovell, "the bloom is so abundant that the fields in autumn look as though covered with snow."[101] I can vouch for that, and the nectar stores to be had going into winter.

In conclusion, the seed mixes containing these flower species are not cheap, costing on average about $1000.00 an acre, but these are hardy, perennial and native flowers that can provide long bloom times in tough soil conditions. These species are used on surface mine sites, highway rights-of-way, conservation reserve plantings, and other pollinator projects. I would also caution land managers to prepare the ground first, with either three herbicide sprays or a prescribed burn. Otherwise, the investment in flower seed will be a waste of time because Johnson grass may take over. "The Earth may laugh in flowers," sayeth nineteenth century philosopher Ralph Waldo Emerson, but Johnson grass may have the last laugh if proper preparations are not made prior to planting flower seed.

---

[101]Lovell, 63.

CHAPTER FIVE: LAWS
(AUSTRALIA AND U.S.)

Capeweed (*Arctotheca calendula*). S. Glowacki. 2007.

In September 2007, from the vantage point of a window seat in a crop-duster airplane, I looked down at the McKay Harbor in Australia and saw ship after ship waiting to be loaded with coal. I had been traveling for 26 hours and wondered if I was hallucinating. McKay had been a sugar-cane town in the nineteenth century, but transformed itself as an outpost for the fossil fuel industry in the twenty-first century. At that time, the Dalrymple Bay Coal Terminal was (and still is) a premier coal export facility. Dr. Julie Beeby at then-Burton mine, owned by Peabody Coal, LLC, extended an invitation to visit the company sites to my colleague Dr. Alice Jones and me. In a rented car, we made our way to the coal mine sites.

The Burton mine is located in the Australian Outback on former ranch land. Shaggy-leaved eucalyptus trees provided the only greenery in a country struggling with a 12-year drought. Even in such reduced circumstances, eucalyptus trees defy drought. They are, in the words of author Kylie Tennant, the "crowning glory of this country."

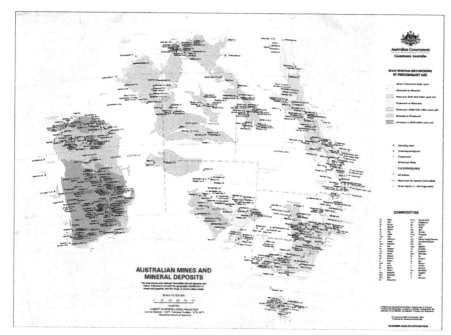

Map of mines and mineral deposits of Australia.

Bench mining, Loy Yang. S. Glowacki. 2007.

Many varieties of eucalyptus exist, and many make exquisite honey. Tennant's experiences as a beekeeper in the Great Depression in 1930s still ring true when she writes of eucalyptus bloom. When eucalyptus bloom, Tennant gushes, "when the great furls of tree-tops look as though they have been showered with snow, their clean scent and color, the way they reflect the hard, hot light, their careless, lopsided, shaggy ugliness, is more than any

L: Mary Bumby, one of the first women to transport her bee hives to New Zealand in 1838, intending to serve as her brother's housekeeper since he was a minister.
R: Eucalyptus tree, (*Eucalyptus salubris*). S. Glowacki. 2007.

graceful precision of gardening. They are creatures of the wilderness, and their flowers...are a foam on the tree's rejoicing."[102]

During our drive in the Outback, Alice and I saw no bloom. We drove west about two hours, and checked into the mine site office first thing in the morning. At that time, many Peabody employees would come to the mine and spend the entire week, sleeping in company dorms, before having a week off to return to their families. Alcohol policies were strictly enforced. At the time, the coal industry was doing well in Australia, with China buying coal mined as quickly as mining companies could transport the coal to the port cities.

In the discussions between our host and Dr. Alice Jones, differences between Australian surface mining laws from United States laws became much clearer. Below are the main differences:

Australia is a socialist country, so landowners have very little input about land decisions until the final stages of a company's decision to mine or not.

Australia has to reclaim to "original approximate *use*" of the land when a coal mining project is finished. This one word "use" is *critically* important and *the* most important difference between the two countries. In the United

[102]Kylie Tennant, *The Honey Flow*, London: Macmillan, 1956, 21

UL: Eucalyptus (*Eucalyptus salubris*), blossom, S. Glowacki. 2007. UR: Eucalyptus plantation. 2007. L: Koala bears feed on eucalyptus trees. This koala mother, a young cub hanging
on tightly to her, had been snacking in a nearby eucalyptus tree and happened to walk in
front of me. My point in including this picture is that eucalyptus trees provide nutrition for an
entire ecosystem in addition to pollinators. Sept. 2007.

States, coal companies have to reclaim to "original approximate *contour.*" A
contour is much more expensive, not necessarily getting the diverse fauna
back on the mine sites, and not necessarily what is best for the environment.
In Australia, which is primarily sheep and cattle country, it is relatively easy
to reclaim to sheep and cattle pasturelands, whereas in the United States, it
can be expensive and difficult, if not impossible in some cases, to reclaim to
original approximately contour.

At the Peabody mine and one that my beekeeper, Stanley Glowacki, worked
in New South Wales, a quickly-growing ground cover called Capeweed (*Arc-
otheca calendula*) is planted to prevent erosion or flooding. Capeweed is a
great pollen producers for honey bees, but in some areas, it can be invasive.

U.S. reclaimed "legacy" mine site, in which compaction of soil was the norm during the 1980s and much of the 1990s. 2012.

Honey bees are not native to Australia or New Zealand. Because the journey was so long, settlers from England had mixed results in successfully transporting hives. Mary Bumby was one of the first women to take her bees to New Zealand in 1838, although few notes remain about her experience with honey bees. In spite of the difficulty beginning that honey bees hives had in being transported to Australia, honey bees soon began to flourish in Australia. In 1842, Elizabeth Macarthur kept bees on her porch and oversaw her merino sheep ranch. Today, the beekeeping industry thrives, profiting from many native eucalyptus trees.[103] Many coal companies replant the surface mine sites with eucalyptus species as soon as the mining is finished. Eucalyptus trees have several advantages, such as being quickly-growing, some species being fire-resistant, and many species producing excellent nectars that cannot be found anywhere else in the world. By the time the visit at Peabody mine site finished, I had become convinced that the phrase "original approximate contour," used in the 1977 Surface Mining Control Reclamation Act, signed in haste by a desperate President Jimmy Carter who wanted to get environmental legislation into law, was problematic and intractable. Understanding that other countries prioritize reclamation to "original approximate use" instead of "original approximate contour" remains a crucial insight, one that

---

[103] Although there are many species of native bees, honey bees were not taken to Australia until the late 1700s.

helps me maintain a "point of reference" that I wish the United States would consider.

Upon return to the United States, I chose to focus on best management practices to supplement the 1977 Surface Mining Control and Reclamation Act, the first legislation written specifically written to address the impact of surface mines by the coal industry.[104] The coal industry had not been used to regulations prior to 1977, and the set of laws were much more about how to control flooding and erosion. According to Dr. Patrick Angel, there were no guidelines for how to control flooding and erosion in 1977, so civilian engineers suggested compaction once mining was finished. Not only would compaction reduce flooding and erosion, it could make commercial development possible by providing flatland in a region devoid of such acreages.

The unintended consequences of this reclamation are still being addressed. In some cases, such as drought when plants cannot grow an extensive root system to hold the soil, compaction did not reduce flooding or erosion, it increased both. While there are some areas that did benefit from the post-mine land uses, such as libraries, schools, bypasses, and community colleges, commercial developers did not flock to the more isolated mine sites, nor did the roads to those areas improve to a degree that could attract, say, residential development. Even as there were notable successes of using "flat land" as commercial development for post-mine use, there were also visible failures of some projects: cracked foundations of hotels and hospital wings fractured after the mine soil settled. Some commercial properties that built hotels or hospital wings had to close their facilities or rebuild.

With these highly visible failures as a backdrop and the plunge in the price of coal in 1995, coal companies approached University of Kentucky foresters to develop another alternative to reclamation, one that emphasized forestry. The collaboration between foresters and coal companies resulted in new approaches and considerations of post-mine land techniques. The Appalachian Regional Reforestation Initiative (1997) evolved as a collection of stakeholders committed to the reduction of soil compaction. This new practice allows tree growth so the roots can control water, improve water quality, and reduce carbon. Another practice advocates adding four feet of topsoil to a mine site prior to reforestation. Trees do well on poor rocky soils, in general, but the

---

[104]The Clark-McNary Act of 1924 made "it much easier for the Forest Service to buy land from willing sellers within predetermined national forest boundaries. It enabled the Secretary of Agriculture to work cooperatively with State officials for better forest protection, chiefly in fire control and water resources. It also provided for continuous production of timber. Additionally, the United States Department of Agriculture (USDA) began working with private forestland owners in reforestation. That was done by broadening the cooperative efforts to include producing and distributing tree seedlings and providing forestry assistance to farmers" (Wikipedia). In *Deforesting the Earth*, Michael Williams credits this act as the primary reason for the "remarkable turnaround from death [of forests] to rebirth after the 1930s." Most significant of all, Williams surmises, is that the lumber companies realized that it was no longer feasible to abandon old plant and move on to new stands (even if there were any) as they had done throughout the nineteenth century. It was cheaper to maintain the expensive capital equipment and its economic and social infrastructure, and replant the surrounding forests." (412).

topsoil gives the seedlings added nutrients and stability. Making sure that trees are planted on a 20-degree slope also enhances tree survival rate.

And more trees, in turn, assist in the reduction of greenhouse gases. According to Mary Booth, an ecologist at Partnership for Public Integrity, "trees are about a quarter carbon, and as they grow (or burn), they bind (or release) about four times their weight in carbon dioxide. For all the hype around carbon-capturing machines, forests are the only proven, scalable technology we have." [105] The Appalachian Regional Reforestation Initiative succeeds in channeling research and energy into reforestation. A nonprofit called Green Forests Work, LLC, emerged from this initiative to coalesce funds, grants, and volunteers under one umbrella to work within Office of Surface Mines and Reclamation to improve best management practices.

Working parallel to the Appalachian Regional Reforestation Initiative, local Kentucky politicians from the coal production counties passed the Pollinator Habitat law and Highway Rights-of-Way law. Both laws promoted the use of pollinator habitat as responsible reclamation for mine sites and highway rights-of-ways. Both laws passed without any dissent, a rarity in Kentucky legislature. When the EPA issued its 2015 federal mandate for all states to create a state-specific pollinator protection plan, these laws came in handy as a starting place for Kentucky stakeholders. The EPA federal mandate was widely considered an "all hands on deck" approach to providing more pollinator habitat, and now as of this writing (2019), the monarch butterfly is on the "watch" list.

Whereas the Kentucky laws addressed challenges in creating more habitat for beekeepers in accessible areas, West Virginia passed a "beekeeper immunity" law in the same year (2010), becoming the first state in the nation to pass a law freeing beekeepers from liability for ordinary negligence. Drafted by Judge Dan O'Hanlon, this law came about as a result of strong support by the leadership of both the House and Senate. At that time, the State Senate President was Earl Ray Tomblin, whose father was a beekeeper. It also helped that House Speaker Richard Thompson was raised by a grandfather who was a beekeeper.

In place for almost a decade now, the West Virginia law requires that beekeepers register their hives and mandates the West Virginia Department of Agriculture define Best Management Practices for beekeepers. All beekeepers who abide by these two provisions will have absolute civil immunity from ordinary negligence. Governor Joe Manchin signed the bill into law on April 1, 2010, making this the first state to protect its beekeeping industry from liability concerns.

---

[105]Elbein.

No state nor nation is immune from economic downturns. Both Appalachia and Australia are witnessing severe changes in the coal industry. In 2015, Michelle Innis wrote in the *New York Times*, an article about Dunedoo, Australia (New South Wales). The article, titled "Coal Mining's Promise Falls Through for Remote Australian Town," indicates how in 2008, the government bought up 177 square miles, boarding up 114 farms/homes, with promises of coal becoming the predominate economic engines. By 2013, the government had abandoned the plan to attract a coal company because of historically-low prices for coal. Many families, some of whom had been in Dunedoo for four generations and had been respected sheep ranchers, have no options. A $5.6 million dollar transition fund exists, but does not do anything to promote agriculture or industry.

Whether beekeeping could thrive in the place of sheep industry or coal industry is a question that I do not think has ever been fully explored in Australia. Australia certainly has unique honey varietals, but the unpredictable rainfall is a persistent challenge for honey producers. Wildfires and floods are also perennial problems affecting Australian honey production.

For both Australia and United States, the answers to economic downturns may not be more legislation or better technology, but reforestation. In Australia, the Great Barrier Reef shows marked decline from the years of increased ocean traffic to its harbors. These reforestation projects in Australia are just beginning and are using the Green Forests Works, LLC, model as their basis for improving water quality in the Great Barrier Reef areas. Here in the United States, people joke that the autumn olive (*Elaeagnus spp.*) is now the state tree of Kentucky and West Virginia.

As my time in Australia was winding down, I presented at the Bees for Rural Development program at 2007 Apimondia International Bee Congress, held in Melbourne. Unbeknownst to me at the time, this conference would shape my interests in Australia and India. I was on a panel with Kunal Sharma, whose uncle had been a manager of a coal company in India, and on an Apimondia technical tour, Stan Glowacki shared his photos of the Loy Yang mine site in New South Wales, leading to a more in-depth approach at beekeeping on surface mine sites. The friendships cemented the similarities that Appalachia shares with India and Australia. No matter what continent my two feet stand, I have come to realize this: we cannot legislate our way out of the current pollinator crisis: we have to "habitat" our way out of it.

CHAPTER SIX: DIVERSE HONEY HUNTER COMMUNITIES (INDIA)

In 2007, India was fourth in terms of world's coal reserves, much of which lay in land under World UNESCO Heritage protection for the unique flora, fauna, and indigenous honey hunter tribes that live in the region. Environmentalist and co-author of *Honey Trails: Honey Hunters in the Blue Mountains* Kunal Sharma was on a panel in Australia at the 2007 Apimondia International Bee Congress, discussing beekeeping as rural development. His uncle had been a coal mining official in India. When Kunal Sharma visited a surface mine site with me in Kentucky in 2012, he discussed the differences between coal mines in India compared to Kentucky. Many environmental safeguards such as air monitors and water quality monitors were not in place in India, leading to levels of dust that "can be seen thirty miles away," said Sharma.

L: Kunal Sharma's uncle, a coal mine executive, K. Sharma.
R: Kunal Sharma, author of *Honey Hunting in the Blue Mountains*, on a visit to Eastern KY and the Red River Gorge, October 2012.

Sharma and co-author Snehlata Nath's book provides insight into the inter-twined relationships of the honey hunters and their use of beeswax and hon-ey as currency to "pay" for services such as making clothes for a wedding ceremony, or preparing food for a funeral, or other types of civil services that must be performed but in a barter economy. Beeswax and honey are the "cash," and if the land and flowers in which the bees that make beeswax and honey is destroyed, then the framework by which the indigenous people (with two million people belonging to over thirty different communities in the Blue Hills) will have to fundamentally change, converting to a cash society, for instance. Deforestation could upend quickly the diverse honey-hunting communities in the Blue Mountains of India.

The Blue Hills are in the Nilgiri district, and once, the area's trees were so remarkable that British explorer wrote in 1830 that they were "strong, wild, and beautiful." One explorer said, "we discovered trees of such enormous height and magnitude, that I am fearful of mentioning my ideas of their mea-surement."[106]

By 1865, the British writer Clements Markham lamented, "a great change has come over the forest-clad mountain districts, in the establishment of many

---

[106]Michael Williams, *Deforesting the Earth*, 362.

UL: A truck hauling coal. K. Sharma.
UR: A map of the Nilgiri region in India. K. Sharma.
L: A tea plantation in the Nilgiri region, photo from Nilgiri Government of Tamilnadu Tour-ism website: https://nilgiris.nic.in/tourist-place/avalanche-ooty/

English planters . . . In all, a total area of 180,000 acres of forest had been cleared for coffee, tea, and chinchona plantations."

When coffee trees suffered a blight, the planters simply switched to tea plantations. Even as the deforestation was taking place, British rulers told themselves that they were making the lives of indigenous people better by offering incomes and steady supplies of food.

Railroads too were another major cause for deforestation in India. The peak of railroad construction saw the deforestation rate double between 122,000 and 130,000 acres per year in the years of 1890s and 1900s. In all, according to Michael Williams, about 700,000 acres of forest must have been destroyed to supply the railroad ties, a sizable amount in one way, but a mere pinprick (about 4.5 percent) of the total destruction of 6 million hectares by agriculture over the same period.[107]

When World War II was consuming the world's resources in Europe, India did not escape the reach of that global war. In addition to its men, India's timber resources fueled the war effort on behalf of the Allies. According to Yasmin Khan in India at War: The Subcontinent and the Second World War, "timber from the forests of Burma and from the northeast and central India was hewn into packing cases, ammunition boxes, railway sleepers, and telegraph poles ... A few voices spoke up for the preservation of the forests but they went unheard."[108]

Inevitably, given the unstable soil structure after such deforestation in India, Australian eucalyptus trees were imported to provide stability in erosion and flooding. However, because eucalyptus trees are considered an invasive tree that absorbs all water in the vicinity, India began an extensive eucalyptus-eradication effort in 2008.

The shame of such massive deforestation is that The Nilgiri Biosphere Reserve is noted for its biodiversity. The area is approximately 5,520 square miles. Within this space, more than 3,700 plant species and 684 vertebrate species (among which 156 are endemic) have been registered. The communities have placed great value on honey and beeswax. When communities need to share resources during a wedding, the transactions often depend upon beeswax or honey. Communities specialize in trades, such as clothing. Or music. Or cooking. If a woman is getting a married, one vendor from a community may provide the clothing, but she will pay that person in beeswax. That vendor will then pay another community to provide food for a feast. At the bottom of this interconnected economic web are the honey hunters who will scale the cliffs to find where the honey bees have built their combs under rock cliffs.

[107]Michael Williams, Deforesting the Earth: From Prehistory to Global Crisis, Chicago: U of Chicago, 360.
[108]Yasmin Khan, India at War: The Subcontinent and the Second World War, Oxford: Oxford UP, 2015, 84-85.

L: A graph showing diversity in Nilgiri region. K. Sharma.
R: Kurinji (*Strobilanthes kurinji*) flower. K. Sharma.

Many native trees and flowers produce nectar for the honey bees. Of these flowers, the powder-blue kurinji (*Strobilanthes kurinji*) flower is a highly-sought after nectar source in the Nilgiri Hills. Beekeepers will drive from miles away to put their bees on these flowers during their bloom season. Its color is why this region is called, "The Blue Mountains."

Deforestation threatens this ancient honey hunting society. The Forest Act of 1865 was supposed to be "the first step towards a rule of property for the forests of British India." Yet, the act ended up creating more friction between British officials and rural people, in part because it was perceived by British officials as offering tenuous control of the continent's forests. A stricter form of legislation was finally passed in 1878 that took into account the type of forest, the applicability of the legislation, and local tenure.[109] In the end, according to Michael Williams, "one is left with a terrible paradox. An admirable and massive administrative edifice had been constructed for the rational use of the timber resource, which had no parallel in the world at this time or for decades to come. It was one of the administrative jewels in the Imperial Crown, a model for the rest of the world. But it was also going to prove to be one of the festering sores in the body of the Indian subcontinent that has still not healed.[110]

It remains to be seen if India will move forward with mining its rich seams of coal, or if it will choose a more environmentally-sensitive path forward. One thing is certain, however. As the planet heats up, more people will want

[109]Williams, 368.
[110]Williams, 368-369.

the conveniences of a life that many Americans take for granted. According to Richard Rhodes in a recent *New York Times* article, "four billion people in Asia will install air conditioners. They will both need them and have a moral right to them."[111] India has treasured its honey hunters for centuries, but it is leap-frogging into the future, and it may inadvertently leave its bees and beekeepers behind.

---

[111]Richard Rhodes, review of *A Bright Future: How Some Countries have solved Climate Change and the Rest Can Follow* by Joshua S. Goldstein and Staffan A. Qvist, *New York Times Book Review*, Feb.5, 2019.

TECO Kids event, ARRI staff, 2012

CHAPTER SEVEN:
COAL COUNTRY BEEWORKS
(KENTUCKY)

On Arbor Day 2008, after negotiating a surface use agreement, four apiaries were established in Perry and Leslie counties, with trees being planted on the slopes behind us.[112] The benefactors Ed and Elaine Holcombe had driven from Tennessee, the Pennsylvania state apiarist Craig Cella had driven from Pennsylvania, Patrick Angel had defended his dissertation and the entire ERI team drove over to unload bee hives and plant trees. Don Gibson and I wanted the apiaries to be teaching apiaries and to be available for ten years because it takes that long to "grow" both a tree and a beekeeper. I put into practice what I had learned at the Australian Apimondia, to restructure education so that the young and young-at-heart apply what they learn to the land around them. By 2014, Coal Country Beeworks had seven apiaries scattered throughout Eastern Kentucky. Below are some bullet points that may be helpful to others considering a similar collaborative project:

Draw up a surface use agreement with the landowner prior to moving beehives on site. In this agreement, spell out locations (using GPS latitude/longitude), fences (who pays for the fence? Who has the key?), road maintenance, expectations regarding honey, etc. Also consider emergency contact information. How is the forage? Can you as the beekeeper plant forage for the honey bees? If bears are in the area, do not move hives until fences are established.

---

[112]VICCO stands for Virginia Iron Coke and Coal Organization.

This apiary shows the goldenrod planted behind the TECO site. This site was used to teach queen production and was my queen-breeding yard.

U: This photo shows the basic setup with which Coal Country Beeworks started: ten hives, a bear-proof fence, new equipment, and seedlings planted on some slopes about a quarter-mile away. L: The Thunder Ridge site is an older mine site compared to the Vicco site, with contour mining happening around it, which left mature vegetation including a honey locust tree. Both apiaries were used to provide workshops on queen production and varroa mite treatments.

TECO, Kids event, J. Bryant. 2013.

Make a "dream" budget. Put *everything* in this budget. Do not be alarmed if it tops a million dollars. Having a budget does not mean you have to spend a million dollars, but it gives you a way to structure your priorities. If that includes a flat-bed truck, then put it in there. Ditto, a forklift. What about medications for the hives? Do not forget to add the costs of queens and queen replacements and varroa mite treatments. Be sure to include the costs of attendance to at least one national or regional conference per year and the cost of one trade journal. Continual education will pay for itself in the long run.

Write grants. More grants for bee-related projects exist now than in 2008. Before the Great Recession, I had to have eight grants in the pipeline for every one grant that was funded. Then, the Great Recession hit, and that number rose to fifteen grants for every one that was funded. I had, on average, about six in the pipeline, ranging from federal to state to private foundation grants. I applied for grants that were over a million dollars, I applied for grants that were only $100.00. I also did not apply for grants for which I was not qualified. For instance, I didn't waste my time chasing grants to "solve Colony Collapse Disorder." I wanted to improve habitat, so I saved myself time by having a clear-cut mission.

Create a timeline. What are the first year goals? What are the 5-year goals? What are the 10-year goals? These goals become "points of reference" to fo-

TECO Kids event, J. Bryant, 2013

cus your activities. To borrow a metaphor from the forest: the first three years of a tree's growth are underground in the root system, where progress is not seen. Progress may not be visible for three to five years, so having goals can help you, as the project coordinator, stay on track and not get discouraged.

Ask, don't tell. This piece of advice is from Robert Watts, long-time caretaker of Lilley Cornett Woods in Letcher County, KY. It works for other situations in life as well. Many corporations have to answer to stakeholders or federal regulators. The idea of providing pollinator habitat can be an issue with some companies who fear that by providing floral resources, their employees may be at more risk for honey bee stings than in other environments. Some corporations may not have the extra money needed for flower seed, which can be exponentially more expensive than grass seed. Some corporations want to see what their competitors do, and see if they can improve on the process. In any event, a "no" is not always a "no" forever. If the request is turned down, accept it and continue to work with the corporations that have permission to move forward with the pollinator projects.

Most importantly, enjoy this work. This point should be the first. If I had waited until retirement to start Coal Country Beeworks, I would have missed one of the most compelling chapters of my life. To give a sense of how quickly the coal industry declined, consider the following statistics:

• In 2008, Kentucky extracted 1.5 billion tons of coal and employed 38,000 jobs, paying $60,000-80,000 plus benefits.

• By 2013, coal production dropped to 862 million tons, with 28,000 paying jobs.

Thunder Ridge, Kids event, C. Bishop. 2013.

• In 2014, the year I became the Kentucky State Apiarist, the Mine Safety and Health Administration estimated that there were 4,000 jobs. Alpha, Inc. shares were approximately .40 cents in 2015 compared to $100.00 in 2008.

• England, the birthplace of the Industrial Revolution in Yorkshire, closed the Kellingley (The Big K) in December 2015. England now imports coal from Russia and U.S.

It has become blood-sport to fixate on the decline of Appalachia, but I continue to see opportunities that have been in the shadows for decades. With best management practices related to reforestation an option now, local beekeepers are excited about beekeeping in a region and with honey imports at an all-time high depressing the market, we can continue to educate in Appalachia about apiculture, silviculture on nectar-producing trees, and knowledge-based industries. In the meantime, the "foodie-culture" continues to become solid and not only do consumers care about local food, they want to support local beekeepers. There is a growing awareness in Kentucky about how much honey is imported from China (some of which has contaminants). In 2019, Kentucky recently implemented a Kentucky Certified Honey Producer program to help consumer discern which honeys are produced from plants rooted in Kentucky soil. In setting the foundation of a forest-based beekeeping industry, I am pleasantly surprised to see how far our state has come. To quote the Irish, "It won't be as long as it's been."

CHAPTER EIGHT: BUDGETS, CONTRACTS, GRANTS

Before there were "GoFundMe" accounts and "Kickstarter" fundraising campaigns, there were organizations that existed to help fund the arts, education, environment, health sectors, human services and public welfare. In fact, most higher education institutions have foundations from which it can support unique projects that differ from conventional "academic track" activities. When I left the academic track in 2007, I entered this less-visible, but *no less important* world, that universities call "external programs" or "sponsored programs." For six years, the university staff helped me navigate the world of federal grants, corporate contracts, and private gifts in an effort to keep funds supporting Coal Country Beeworks because it was blended education, environment, regional stewardship and economic development together.

At the beginning of this book, I mentioned the importance of gifts. The Edwin and Elaine Holcombe gift launched Coal Country Beeworks in 2008, which generated a modest stipend while I continued to work with coal companies to develop surface use agreements and apply for other grants. If a gift is granted through a university foundation, the university has protocols in place. The money cannot have strings attached by the donor. Also, students have to benefit from the gift in some way. In some cases, universities will charge an overhead fee, so that the incidental expenses such as computers, electricity, office space, etc. are covered.

To give a broader perspective on charitable gifts, recent statistics by the World Giving Index lists the United States as fourth in the world, according to the Charity Aid Foundation. Two categories that stand out in terms of monetary gifts are the health sector, which accounts for 70% of annual gifts or $1.4 trillion in gifts, and education, which accounts for 18% or $354 billion in total revenues. In 2017, private giving from individuals, foundations, and businesses totaled $410 billion.[113] O'Daniel's assessment is that the generous support also suggests a deep skepticism of government or institutional spending, i.e., that people realize that there are "gaps" that are not acknowledged by institutional hierarchy. This is precisely where the program Coal Country Beeworks "fit" in. As long as I brought in the funds, the university would provide infrastructure to address a national crisis impacting pollinators.

---

[113]Kris O'Daniel, "We're a nation of charity: What that says about us, Government," Lexington Herald-Leader, Opinion, 9A, May 4, 2019.

Thus began my world of writing grants. I had no pride and still do not when I need to raise funds for pollinators. With every grant I submitted, I became more astounded at the world of nonprofits. According to O'Daniel, "The Internal Revenue Service registered over 1.6 million organizations as nonprofits all contributing an estimated $985 billion to the U.S. economy and employing more than 10% of the domestic work force."

The Kentucky Foundation for Women awarded a grant for $3000.00, which was used to pay for girls' bee suits, an observation hive, which is still used ten years later. See link: http://www.kfw.org/

The Steele-Reese Foundation that awarded funding for two years, including salary and travel. This private foundation, founded by Eleanor Steele and Emmet Reese, provided vital support for me to be able to provide teaching opportunities to beekeepers. Eleanor Steele had been a classically trained opera singer who decided to go to Idaho after a stint in Europe: her purpose was to escape people. Emmet Reese left Eastern Kentucky and decided to go to Idaho. The two met, married, and built one of the finest cattle operations in Idaho. Their legacy was to leave a foundation that would help the people from where they resided: Its criteria appealed to me, being an organization that advises applicants to "be modest but direct in aim": http://steele-reese.org/

One of the first activities I did in 2009 was work with Phil Craft and Charles May to start the Eastern Kentucky Winter Bee School, a one-day multi-track beekeeping program. I have reached out to the Foundation for Appalachian Kentucky for small grants to offset hotel rooms for speakers, since many must travel from over two hours away to speak at the school in Perry County, KY. For more details about this Foundation, see the following link: https://www.appalachianky.org/

Kentucky is fortunate to have been part of tobacco diversification settlement in the 1990s. As a result, there are funds dispersed through the Governor's Office of Agriculture Policy. This office created the Kentucky Agriculture Development Board (KADB) and this board meets twice a month to consider grant applications and/or approve loans. In the past ten years, the KADB has approved four different beekeeping-based grants. Two have been for queen bee production grants, one for a Kentucky Certified Honey Producer program, and one for a county beekeeping mentoring program. There is even a pool of funds for youth to get started in agriculture. The terms are more limited, such as youth cannot borrow more than $5,000.00 and must have a parent of FFA or 4-H leader co-sign, but a kid can go a long way with that type of start-up. More about these types of grants and loans can be found at this website: https://agpolicy.ky.gov/Pages/default.aspx.

As the State Apiarist, I write grants on a regular basis. With Green Forests Work team, we worked on a USDA-NRCS grant to reclaim legacy mine sites, planting trees that would attract the threatened cerulean warblers (*Setophaga cerulea*). As it so happens, some of the tree species are great nectar and pollen producers. Five states participated in this grant application that was awarded 8 million dollars over four years. I receive no salary from this particular grant, but just by providing in-kind services such as beekeeping workshops, I reinforced the fact that trees are a crop, and the Kentucky Department of Agriculture is as serious about silviculture as it is about agriculture. Approximately 100,000 farms in Kentucky have over ten acres, and much of that territory is wooded. If these family farmers are able to use their trees as part of forest-based beekeeping, I've expanded the initial mission of Coal Country Beeworks.

In 2017, Purdue University successfully applied for a USDA-Critical Agriculture and Research Extension grant. The funds for this type of grant support research that can have immediate impacts to agriculture. Due to Dr. Greg Hunt's research on mite-bite queens, he was awarded this grant, ranking first out of all the proposals. Each state he included, such as Illinois, Ohio, Kentucky, West Virginia, and Michigan received a modest amount of funding to start a queen production association. In my state, it is the Kentucky Queen Bee Breeders Association. And for three years, each state has received approximately $4,500.00 to provide queen production workshops. Fortunately, the Kentucky Queen Bee Breeders Association has been able to use that Purdue grant as a match from the Kentucky Agriculture Development Board in 2019 and is able to provide direct-apiary consultation to queen bee producers to select and assess for mite-chewing behavior.

Landowners can also apply for federal pollinator habitat grants with the Farm Services Agency and the Natural Resources Conservation Service. The key difference between the Conservation Reserve Program and the EQIP has to do with the land's purpose prior to pollinator habitat. If land was productive farmland, the landowner will want to work with the FSA and CRP. See the following link: https://www.fsa.usda.gov/programs-and-services/conservation-programs/conservation-reserve-program/

For the socially disadvantaged, there is a form called CCC-860. If an individual qualifies as socially disadvantaged, (minorities, first-time farmers, for instance), there are some perks, such as discounts on emergency livestock insurance, etc. See the following link: https://forms.sc.egov.usda.gov/efcommon/eFileServices/eFormsAdmin/CCC0860_140402V01.pdf

If the landowner has some areas that are not productive farmland, that person should go to the NRCS and see if EQIP funding can offset flower seeds. See the following link: https://www.nrcs.usda.gov/wps/portal/nrcs/main/national/programs/financial/eqip/. Landowners need to budget about $1,000.00 an acre in terms of herbicide spraying, flower seed invoices, and preparation (building "prescribed burn" brakes, for example).

Writing a grant and creating a business plan have many similarities: a time-line, a methodology, a budget, and a mission or set of goals for why the action is important. It takes as much work to apply for a smaller amount of funds, in some cases, as it does to apply for larger amounts of funds. I would caution anyone who thinks that grants are "free money" to reconsider that perception. Not only is there accountability, there are countless "un-billable" hours that go into completing a grant. I am not trying to discourage anyone from doing this, but one should realize that if one is going to be on "soft" money, he or she will always be writing grants and then trying to complete them.

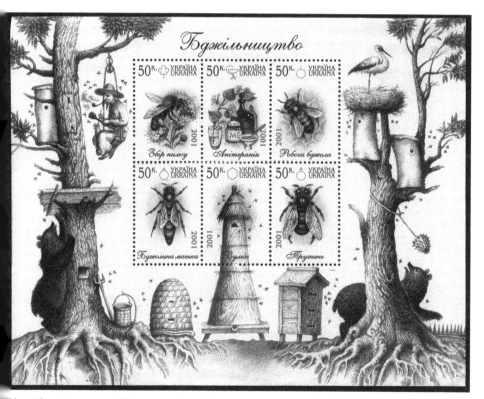

This Ukrainian stamp illustrates a few of the same challenges that exist for Appalachian bee-keepers, primarily bears and the need for a beekeeper to use some type of smoke (i.e., pipe or a smoker).

Chapter Nine: Challenges

There is no straight, linear path to success. In fact, by the time I transitioned to the Kentucky Department of Agriculture, I was no longer sure I even knew what success was. Ten years later, at the time of this writing, the successes are much easier to see and the bruises from the failures have ebbed. This chapter will detail some of the challenges that still exist for anyone who chooses to work on a large-scale forest-based project such as this:

Thefts

Every year when I had hives on surface mine sites, thieves stole over-wintered hives. Presumably, thieves were beekeepers whose own hives died from mismanagement or simply for the thrill of stealing property. One apiary was used for shooting practice, with several hives pierced with high-powered shotgun shells. Even the TECO yard in Jenkins, i.e., the apiary that had the highest and most secure fence, was vandalized. In fact, in some places where trees were planted as part of Arbor Day events, thieves stole the bare-root seedlings.

As the desire for hives continues to exceed demand, thefts will continue to rise. It is not just a problem in Appalachia, but also in California, Texas, and Florida as higher prices for hive rentals means more people are just trying to move boxes into orchards without regard to the bees, the orchards that need pollination, or the beekeepers. Hive theft is an age-old problem. In Egypt, during the Twentieth Dynasty, "archers were appointed to protect "collectors of honey," according to Gene Kritsky in *The Tears of Re*.[114] The Russian historian Dorothy Galton provides evidence in her *Survey of a Thousand Years of Beekeeping in Russia*, that the code of Alexis Mikhaylovich in 1649 details fines to people who steal bees from their neighbors' trees or cut down trees with no respect for tree ownership.[115]

I have already mentioned that in 1978, Patrick Angel had set up an apiary on Tennessee Valley Authority land on a former Peabody mine site. The project did really well, with students from Madisonville Community College learning beekeeping and selling honey as a fundraiser. The project ended with vandalism. It is difficult to have hives survive the winter, only to return to a yard and see it stolen. Worse, the beekeeper cannot just go to a hardware store and

---

[114]Gene Kritsky, *The Tears of Re*, Oxford: Oxford UP, 77.
[115]Dorothy Galton, *Survey of a Thousand Years of Beekeeping in Russia*, Gerrards Cross: International Bee Research Association, 1971, 31.

Bear damage, S. Buckley, 2018.

buy more hives. So, the thief is really stealing three years from the beekeeper, i.e., this year's hives, next year's hives, and finally by the third year, the beekeeper can make a honey crop.

Theft was one of the more unpleasant aspects of this project, and I do not miss that aspect of the project. The Hawaiian term for theft, i.e., "taxing," was useful for me to remember in these circumstances. In some years, I was "taxed" heavier than others. In a country that doesn't have insurance for agricultural theft, those losses came from my grants and pocket and illustrate yet one more way that the federal government does not seriously understand agriculture.

BEARS

Just as with theft, bears are a perennial problem if hives are in an unprotected area. In medieval times, Ukrainian beekeepers used to place their hives in the tops of trees to keep the hives (and themselves) safe. If the beekeeper does not establish a fence before the hives are moved onsite, the beekeeper risks not just the loss of the beehives, but also the future ones that the bears will "revisit" later. A beekeeper cannot build a fence high enough after a bear has established where a beehive is. In Kentucky, there are nuisance laws established by Kentucky Fish and Wildlife to help beekeepers build fences. There are also license permits if a bear gets too close to an established home. But there are no funds to help a beekeeper recoup hive loss to bears, something that the federal insurance laws should consider adding.

See Addendum for Pennsylvania bee inspector Craig Cella's directions on building a bear-proof fence.

DISEASES

Diseases are a fact of beekeeping. After I became the state apiarist, the university did not fill my position for four months. During this time, the university apiaries sat neglected. By the time my replacement had been hired, the apiaries suffered a very contagious disease called American foulbrood. In my new role as apiarist, I had to burn the majority of the hives, bees, equipment, etc.

However, something good came out of the apocalyptic nightmare: I reached out to Dr. Sandra Hope and she sent me some of her "trial" phages. A phage is a naturally-occurring virus that attacks bacteria. Phages have been around for millions of years and are plentiful in many environments (and thus, relatively affordable). As a control for American foulbrood, a phage adheres to a bacteria wall. The phage inserts its genetic code into the American foulbrood bacteria, and replicates its code into the American foulbrood bacteria until the cell wall eventually disintegrates, leaving no residue nor creating conditions in which the bacteria builds resistance (as can happen with antibiotics). These phages were applied to hives not showing any symptoms in 2015.

I established a quarantine area in my own apiary. I shook the hives not showing any symptoms into new equipment and then sprayed everything with phages mixed with sugar syrup. I am happy to report that we did not see any American foulbrood after this happened. There is now a product called Broodsafe: www.broodsafe.com.

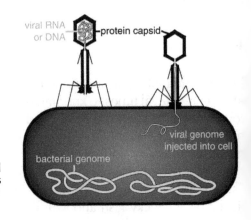

Broodsafe is a phage-based product that is now available to beekeepers to control the bacteria causing American foulbrood. A phage is a virus to the bacteria, occurs naturally, and leaves no chemicals in the beeswax nor can the American foulbrood bacteria develop resistance. It can be applied in sugar syrup or as a powder, but will not work on any of the other brood diseases such as European foulbrood, chalkbrood or sacbrood.

Small hive beetles were not a major issue on surface mine sites for me. Perhaps it was because of soil compaction or perhaps it was because I eventually started using strips of black conveyor belt known as "coal black," that had outlived its usefulness on the line. For whatever reason, small hive beetles were not much of a problem in my apiaries from 2008-2014.

I also caution beekeepers that simply placing their hives on adequate forage is not enough. Every single acre in the U.S. could be planted with a perfect rotation of flowers, but if the beekeeper does not monitor for varroa mite loads, or queen loss, or disease, the beekeeper will still have high hive losses. It is not enough to have plenty of flowers; the beekeeper has to be monitoring for diseases and problems on a regular basis.

TREES

As much as I loved the sourwood species, I learned soon enough that it does not "fit" with the current reforestation templates. I am not the only one to learn this humbling lesson. Western states such as California have spent a vast amount of time and money creating "pines in lines," a type of reforestation plan that "plants" pine trees just like a row crop, only to realize that "the wrong reforestation polices can be worse than no reforestation polices at all."[116]

The problems have been numerous: planting some species in "plantation style," such as the "pines in lines" approach in Western states, has meant when a wildfire burns though, as happened in Fort McMurray, Alberta Canada, the black spruce trees were not mature (high) enough to "weather" the flames, and the immature trees became fuel instead. Furthermore, the black spruce "gorged themselves" on the groundwater that existed in the swamps, and as the land dried, the trees grew into enormous stores of fuel.

A good reminder is best stated by Sofi Faruqi, a forest economist. "If you take the approach that no matter what, more trees are better, that's going to have unintended consequences.[117] Restoration policy can no longer fail to address what kind of trees are being planted, or how it jibes with the larger health of the forest, the amount of water available, or the needs of the local people."

Finally, having a diverse tree list is important for those years in which some species have "off" years and are not available. Or even better, perhaps OSMRE officials will begin leaving some of these areas that do not directly humans and communities alone so that the forest can begin to re-establish itself on its own time frame. The "founder stand" approach is used in Latin America and

---

[116]Saul Elbein, "How to Regrow a Forest: Get out of the way," National Geographic, April 26, 2019. www.nationalgeographic.com/2019/04/how-to-regrow-forest-right-way-minimize-fire-water-use.html.
[117]Elbein.

it involves planting a small grove that is left to grow and seed over time, an idea that to the USDA at one time would have been considered "heretical."[118] It is worth remembering that left alone, Appalachian forests can regenerate themselves very quickly. I am not advocating a complete reversal of post-mine land use control, after all, I *remember* the years in Harlan County prior to 1997, when as a child, I would see deep furrows eroded into mountains.

However, I am advocating more options: seed collection is just as important, and perhaps as successful, as planting seedlings.

More funding to help local-level farms and small-start ups take advantage of the opportunities of a forest-based beekeeping industry would also help overcome some of the start-up challenges. After all, hives do not produce honey in their first years. At this point in time, there is simply not enough money to help with local initiatives and the tailored education that beekeeping requires. Even as I write this, a bill titled RECLAIM (Revitalizing the Economy of Coal Communities by Leveraging Local Activities and Investing More) that would bring $100 million to Kentucky's coal communities passed the U.S. House Committee on Natural Resources and will advance to the full House of Representatives. The bill would pay for the reclamation of abandoned mine lands and foster economic growth. It is not the first time the bill has been up for a vote. It failed in 2016, and then in 2017. It has not been without its critics, who call it a "boondoogle," citing the need for reduced regulation instead of taxpayer funded local initiatives.[119]

[118]Elbein.
[119]Will Wright, "Bill that Promises $100 Million for KY Coal Communities Gets Another Chance," Lexington Herald-Leader, A3-4, May 3, 2019.

CHAPTER TEN: CONCLUSION

As of 2019, land use continues to be a primary cause of insect decline, including honey bees. Turf grass is the number one crop grown in the United States. According to Mark Bitman in 2013, "it's our biggest crop, three times as big as corn, according to research done using a variety of data, much of it from satellites. That's around a trillion square feet — 50,000 square miles." The chemicals needed to sustain the turf grass, the fuel needed to mow it, the labor needed to control it are all elements of a culture that has lost touch with reality.

Extractive mining has a major impact on pollinator habitat too. Reforestation offers some methods and species to promote insects, but the true impact of these efforts will not be known for at least five-ten years. According to Ohio State professor Gabriel Karn, "mitigation is not reclamation" in some areas. The efforts that benefit some species may not apply to other species. His lecture focused on snakes and gas pipeline rights-of-way in Ohio, but one could easily have substituted pollinators. What benefits one pollinator, such as a honey bee, may not benefit the bumble bees at all.[120]

[120]Gabriel Karn, "Vegetation Management and Rights-of-Way," University of Kentucky, March 27, 2019. Public lecture.

Sourwood (*Oxydendrum arboretum*) trees started from seed. 2012.

Photo of sourwood (*Oxydendrum arboretum*), started from seeds. 2012.

Companies that maintain rights-of-way habitat show promise for beekeepers too. With Columbia Gas owning 41,000 miles in six states, vegetation managers are assessing low-growing ground cover crops in an effort to make it easier for the ground crews to find gas leaks, but also to reduce mowing and make it easier for pollinators to find nutrition.

Not only is Columbia Gas committed to providing pollinator habitat, it is partnering with the Kentucky Transportation Cabinet to convert areas where pipelines and highway rights-of-way overlap. This is an exciting opportunity for the region and represents the long-term commitment of corporate sponsors to this effort to help insects.

I once was asked if I am optimistic about our efforts to help reverse pollinator declines, and my answer was, and is, a cautious "yes." Our nation repeatedly has shown itself capable of reversing declines, such as the rapid mobilization to protect the bald eagle, the gray wolf, and Florida alligators. Yet I am also under no illusions that humans have created enormous pressures for insects and less-visible species, and as a civilization, progress for protection of insects has been slow. We are living in an uncontrolled experiment of rising temperatures, more uncontrolled chemical products in the environment and few educational resources about how to use those products responsibly. An infrastructure by which pollinator habitat has been happening through a hodge-podge of activities, namely, the Pollinator Protection Plans that each state creates, but more systemic approaches are needed for the next ten years.

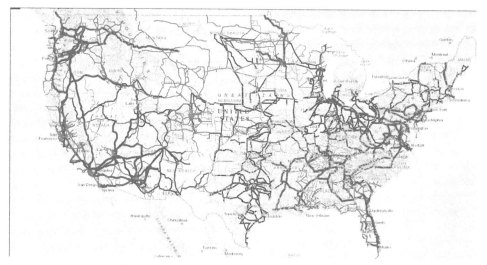

Rights-of-Way map of the United States. ArcGIS.com.
http://www.arcgis.com/home/item.html?id=731256cbe9a04da683e02663da9186ae

People can feel helpless when faced with the enormity of insect loss. Yet, there is much that one person can do. For the past ten years, I have picked up a tree spade in spring, the pliant bare-root seedling in my hands, its vulnerable root cap barely visible in the rock. Now, five years, the tree is taller than I am, converting carbon dioxide into breathable air, and into its flower, a bee will duck its head, slurping nectar and tucking pollen into its back legs. The Earth may "laugh in flowers," but we breathe with trees and feast with bees.

Kentucky Department of Transportation, I-71 south plot, 2018.

BIBLIOGRAPHY

Aldenderfer, Amy. "Winter is for Witchhazel," University of Kentucky Horticulture newsletter, Nov. 2015. www.uky.edu/hort/.

Angel P.N. and C.M. Christensen. 1976. "Honey Production on Reclaimed Strip Mine Soil." p. 708-711, in: Hill Lands: Proceedings of an International Symposium. West Virginia University, Morgantown.

Arnold, Chester, "The Fossil-Plant Record." *Aspects of Palynology: An Introduction to Plant Microfossils in Time.* Eds: Robert Tschudy and Richard Scott. New York: Wiley Interscience, 1969.

Bittman, Mark. "Lawns into Gardens," *New York Times,* Jan. 29, 2013, Opinion. https://opinionator.blogs.nytimes.com/2013/01/29/lawns-into-gardens/?auth=login-email

Cannon, W.B. *The Wisdom of the Body: How the Human Body Reacts to Danger and Maintains the Stability Essential to Life,* Norton, 1932.

Caron, Dewey and Lawrence John Connor. *Honey Bee Biology and Beekeeping.* Kalamazoo MI: Wicwas, 2013.

Castle, Stephen. "Lights Out in Britain for the Coal Industry," *New York Times,* Nov.1, 2015.

Cella, Craig. "How to Live with Black Bears," *American Bee Journal* 6 (2005): 479-482.

Collison, Clarence. "Pollen Consumption and Digestion, *Bee Culture,* Feb. 16, 2017. https://www.beeculture.com/a-closer-look-7/

Ibid. "Pollen Quality," *Bee Culture,* April 23, 2016. https://www.beeculture.com/pollen-quality/

Dennis, Brian and William P. Kemp. "How Hives Collapse: Allee Effects, Ecological Resilience, and the Honey Bee." PLOS ONE, 2016; 11 (2): e0150055 DOI: 10.1371/journal.pone.0150055

Galton, Dorothy. *Survey of a Thousand Years of Beekeeping in Russia.* Garrards Cross: International Bee Research Association, 1971.

Elbein, Saul. "How to Regrow a Forest: Get Out of the Way," National Geographic, April 26, 2019. www.nationalgeographic.com/2019/04/how-to-regrow-forest-right-way-minimize-fire-water-use.html.

Flannery, Tim. *Eternal Frontier: An Ecological History of North America and its Peoples.* London: Vintage, 2001.

Freese, Barbara. *Coal: A Human History.* New York: Penguin, 2003.

Harman, Alan. "Sunflower Pollen seems to cause real problems for *Nosema ceranae.* That's Good," Catch the Buzz, October 18, 2018. https://www.beeculture.com/catch-the-buzz-sunflower-pollen-seems-to-cause-real-problems-for-nosema-ceranae-thats-good/

Hesbach, William. "Winter Management," *Bee Culture,* Oct. 21, 2016. https://www.beeculture.com/winter-management/

Horn Potter, Tammy, Patrick Angel, Carl Zipper, Michael Ulyshen, Michael French, Jim Burger, Mary Beth Adams. "Re-establishing Pollinator Habitat on Mined Lands Using the Forestry Reclamation Approach," Forest Reclamation Advisory #14, Feb. 2017. https://arri.osmre.gov/FRA/Advisories/FRA-14-ReestablishingPollinatorHabitat-Feb2017.pdf

Horn Potter, Tammy and Kunal Sharma. "Honey Corridors in the Nilgiri Biosphere Reserve and Appalachian Coal Production Areas" Global Mountain Regions: Conversations toward the

Future. Eds. Anne Kingsolver and Sasikumar Balasundaram. Bloomington, Indiana UP, 2018. 297-314.

Hubbell, Sue. *A Book of Bees: And How to Keep Them.* New York: Houghton Miflin, 1988.

Innis, Michelle. "Coal Mining's Promise Falls Through for Remote Australian Town," New York Times, Oct. 8, 2015

Kentucky Forest Sector Economic Contribution Report, 2017-2018.   College of Agriculture, Food and Environment, University of Kentucky Forestry Department, 2019.

Khan, Yasmin. *India at War: The Subcontinent and the Second World War.* Oxford: Oxford UP, 2015.

Knebusch, Kurt and Paul Snyder. "Holly Berry," *Bee Culture,* Jan. 23, 2017. https://www.bee-culture.com/holly-bee/

Kritsky, Gene. *The Tears of Re: Beekeeping in Ancient Egypt.* Oxford: Oxford UP, 2015.

Krochmal, Arnold. "Forests as Nectar Sources," *Bee Culture* 114.12 (1986), 640.

Krochmal, Connie. "Native Serviceberries," *Bee Culture,* Feb. 22, 2016. https://www.beecul-ture.com/native-serviceberries/

Ibid, "Persimmons for the Garden," *Bee Culture,* October 15, 2015. https://www.beeculture.com/persimmons-for-the-garden/

Lee, Frederick, Douglas Rusch, Frank Stewart, Heather Mattila, and Irene Newtown. "Saccharaide breakdown and fermentation by the honey bee gut microbiome," Environmental Microbiology, 2014.

Lovell, John. *Honey Plants of North America,* A.I. Root, 1926.

McCleary, Doug. "Reinventing the United States Forest Service: Evolution from Custodial Management, to Production Forestry, to Ecosystem Management." http://www.fao.org/3/ai412e/AI412E06.htm

Meko, Tim. *Six Maps that Show the Anatomy of America's Vast Infrastructure. Washington Post,* Dec. 1, 2016. https://www.washingtonpost.com/graphics/national/maps-of-american-in-frastrucure/?tid=graphics-story

Mickels-Kokwe, Guni. Small-scale Woodland-based Enterprises with Outstanding Economic Potential: The Case of Honey in Zambia. Center for International Forestry Research, Bogor Barat, Indonesia, 2006.

Muir, John. *The Story of My Boyhood and Youth.* Boston and New York: Houghton Miflin, 1913.

Muyskens, John, Dan Keating, and Samuel Granados. *Mapping how the United States Generates Its Electricity. Washington Post,* Originally published July 31, 2015. Updated, March 28, 2017. http://wapo.st/power-plants?tid=ss_mail

O'Brien, Dennis. "Changes in Goldenrod, A Key Source of Honey Bee Nutrition," Catch the Buzz, June 4, 2016. https://www.beeculture.com/catch-buzz-changes-goldenrod-key-source-honey-bee-nutrition/

O'Daniel, Kris. "We're a nation of charity. What that says about us, Government," Lexington Herald-Leader, Opinion 9A, May 4, 2019.

O'Keefe, Jen. *Thirty Common Pollen Types in South East Kentucky.* 2018. Unpublished manuscript.

Powers, Richard. *The Overstory.* New York: Norton, 2018.

Prothero, Daniel. *Evolution of the Earth.* McGraw-Hill. 2003.

Reclaiming the Future: *Reforestation in Appalachia.* DVD. 2008.

Sammataro, Diana and Ann Harman. *Major Flowers Important to Honey Bees in the Northeast and mid-Atlantic States*. Tucson, AZ: AlphaGraphics, 2013. 2nd edition.

Schmidt, Kylie. *Annual Report of Green Forests Work*. https://issuu.com/greenforestswork/docs/2017_annual_report_417812becf0c7e

Schmidt, Kylie. *Angels of Apiculture: Setting the Stage for Healthy Bees, Trees, and Families*: https://drive.google.com/open?id=0B_PqCIyVmpCiOW05bkN4d0g5Rms

Seeley, Tom. *Honeybee Democracy*. Princeton: Princeton UP, 2010.

Segal, David. "The People v. the Coal Baron," *New York Times*, June 21, 2015

Sharma, Kunal and Snehlata Nath. *Honey Trails in the Blue Mountains*. Kotagiri, India: Keystone Foundation, 2007.

Tautz, Jurgen. *The Buzz About Bees: Biology of a Superorganism*. Heidelberg, Germany: Springer-Verlag, 2008.

Trimboli, Shannon. *Honey Plants in the Ohio Valley Region*. Glasgow, KY: Solidago, 2018.

Ibid. "Rough Leaf Dogwood." Post Feb. 26, 2019. www.shannontrimboli.com/rough-leafed-dogwood/

Williams, Michael. *Deforesting the Earth: From Prehistory to Global Crisis*. Chicago: U of Chicago P, 2002.

Wilson, Joseph and Olivia Messinger Carril. *The Bees in Your Backyard: A Guide to North America's Bees*. Princeton: Princeton UP, 2016.

Winston, Mark. *The Biology of the Honey Bee*. Harvard: Harvard UP, 1987.

Winter, Norman. "Coreopsis add light in gardens," *Lexington Herald Leader*, May 12, 2019, 4D.

Wohlleben, Peter. *The Hidden Life of Trees: What They Feel, How They Communicate: Discoveries from a Secret World*. London: HarperCollins. Originally published in Germany, 2015.

Wright, Will. "Bill that Promises $100 Million for KY Coal Communities Gets Another Chance," *Lexington Herald-Leader*, A3-4, May 3, 2019.

"Zambia: Bwana Mkubwa Donates Bee-Keeping Kit to Chief Chiwala's Kansafwe." *Times of Zambia*, January 19, 2005.

Addendum One

Palynology Research Laboratory
Department of Anthropology
Texas A&M University
College Station, TX 77843-4352
(979) 845-5242   FAX (979) 845-4070

Dear Tammy,

I have completed the pollen study of the two honey samples you submitted for analysis. Specific details about the extraction and analysis procedures I used for these samples are identical to those I normally use on other such samples and used on your previous samples. I could repeat these procedures if you wish.

ANALYSIS

Sample Horn:

Your sample would be classified as Unifloral Clover Honey because it is dominated by the pollen (and nectar) from one major source in a percentage greater than 45% (just barely). By definition, which was established more than 50 years ago, a unifloral honey should contain more than 45% pollen and nectar from a single source. There are some exceptions, which I have outlined in my attached paper on pollen coefficients.

As you can see from the table of pollen contents below, your sample is dominated by clover pollen in a percentage of 45.8%. Several major pollen and nectar types are also present including blackberries and sumac/poison ivy. There are also some other minor pollen and nectar types represented in your honey, as noted below in Table 1. These appear to be similar to the same types of pollen and nectar in your previous samples.

The pollen concentration value of just over 59,000 pollen grains per 10 grams of honey is within the normal and expected range for clover honey which can sometimes reach levels of over 100,000 pollen grains per 10 grams of honey.

Sample Snavely:

As you can see in Table 1, this is a multifloral honey because it is not dominated by any one special type of pollen and nectar. Instead it has major pollen and nectar coming from the plants of autumn olive, maples, willows, and various types of plants in the rose family. As I may have mentioned in one of my previous reports, the biggest problem with pollen in the rose family is that there are over 85 different genera and more than 3,000 different species in that family. In the state of Kentucky there are at least 100 different species in the rose family. Each of those species produces a "unique" pollen type but ALL OF THE TYPES look extremely similar, which makes precise identification very difficult without the higher resolution possible using a scanning electron microscope. There are a few genera we can identify (Rubus, Prunus) but for example Malus (apples) pollen and Crataegus (hawthorn) pollen look nearly identical and each genus contains a number of species each of which looks slightly different from the other species. I have no doubt that some of them in this honey sample are from Amelanchier (service berry) but it is difficult to be certain.

There is also an unknown type in this sample that I have not seen before, or if I have I don't remember seeing it. It looks like a clover, but I can't be certain. As you know there are over 100 species and varieties just of Trifolium. Although most clover species look similar there are variations among them. In short, I could not find a good match for the unknown type in this sample.

The pollen concentration value is just over 71,000, which is in Category II. That is the primary category for most of the multifloral honey produced in the United States and thus appears quite normal.

Sincerely,

Vaughn M. Bryant, Jr
Professor and Director

TABLE 1. RELATIVE POLLEN COUNT OF THE HONEY SAMPLES

Horn Honey Samples 2016

POLLEN TAXA	Horn, Lexington	%	Snavely, Eastern KY	%
Acer (maple)	5	2.5%	21	10.1%
Acer rubrum (red maple)	0	0.0%	0	0.0%
ASTERACEAE (dandelion-type)	0	0.0%	1	0.5%
ASTERACEAE (ragweed-type)	0	0.0%	0	0.0%
ASTERACEAE (sunflower-type)	7	3.4%	0	0.0%
BRASSICACEAE (mustard family)	0	0.0%	0	0.0%
Castanea (chestnut, chinkapin)	0	0.0%	0	0.0%
Cephalanthus (buttonbush)	0	0.0%	0	0.0%
Clematis (clematis)	0	0.0%	0	0.0%
Cornus (dogwood)	0	0.0%	11	5.3%
Convolvulus (bindweed)	0	0.0%	0	0.0%
Diospyros (persimmon)	0	0.0%	0	0.0%
Elaeagnus (autumn olive)	0	0.0%	66	31.9%
Fraxinus (ash)	3	1.5%	0	0.0%
Gleditsia (honey locust)	2	1.0%	0	0.0%
Ilex (holly)	0	0.0%	0	0.0%
Juglans (walnut)	2	1.0%	0	0.0%
LILIACEAE (lily family)	0	0.0%	0	0.0%
Ligustrum (privet)	0	0.0%	0	0.0%
Liriodendron (tulip tree)	3	1.5%	0	0.0%
Magnolia (magnolia)	1	0.5%	0	0.0%
Melilotus (clover)	0	0.0%	0	0.0%
Myrica (wax myrtle)	0	0.0%	0	0.0%
Nyssa (gum)	10	4.9%	4	1.9%
Oxydendrum arboreum (sourwood)	0	0.0%	0	0.0%
Parthenocissus (Virginia creeper)	0	0.0%	0	0.0%
Phyla lanceolate (frogfruit)	0	0.0%	0	0.0%
Pinus (pine)	0	0.0%	0	0.0%
Plantago (plantain)	0	0.0%	0	0.0%
Platanus (sycamore)	0	0.0%	1	0.5%
POACEAE (grass family)	1	0.5%	0	0.0%
Prunus (plum, peach, cherry)	0	0.0%	12	5.8%
Quercus (oak)	0	0.0%	7	3.4%
RANUNCULACEAE (buttercups)	2	1.0%	0	0.0%
RHAMNACEAE (buckthorn)	0	0.0%	0	0.0%
ROSACEAE (rose family)	0	0.0%	39	18.8%
Rhus/Toxicodendron (sumac, poison ivy)	27	13.3%	2	1.0%
Robinia (locust)	0	0.0%	0	0.0%
ROSACEAE (rose family)	9	4.4%	0	0.0%
Rubus (blackberry, dewberry)	30	14.8%	0	0.0%
Salix (willow)	4	2.0%	14	6.8%
SCROPHULARIACEAE	0	0.0%	0	0.0%
Tilia (basswood)	0	0.0%	0	0.0%
Trifolium/Melilotus (clover)	93	45.8%	2	1.0%
Ulmus (elm)	0	0.0%	0	0.0%
Vitis (grape)	1	0.5%	0	0.0%
Unknown pollen	3	1.5%	27	13.0%
Totals	**203**	**100.0%**	**207**	**100.0%**
Lycopodium spores counted	63		54	
Pollen conc. per 10 grams of honey	59,878		71,234	

ADDENDUM TWO
BEAR PROOF FENCES

Craig Cella, Pennsylvania Bee Inspector. Article "How to Live with Black Bears," *American Bee Journal* 6 (2005): 479-482.

MATERIALS NEEDED TO CONSTRUCT 16 x 32 FOOT PEN TO HOLD 10+ HIVES

• Fiberglass oilfield rods 1 1/4 inch, 6 feet to make fence posts (from Kencove,1.800.536.2682); 12 posts are needed for each yard, so 36 posts total, and it's best to have a few extra on hand

• 1/4 bolts (stainless steel will work but galvanized is better)

• Zinc-dipped 52-inch Cattle Panels; 6 panels needed for each yard, 18 panels total. (from Behlen Co. Neb. 1.800.447.2751)

• 1 Parmak Magnum solar-power fencer, output 1 joule, per yard (1.800.662.1038 www.parmakusa.com)

Directions (page 481)

• Drive posts 2 feet into the ground—use gloves when handling fiberglass posts

• After driving in the posts, stand a panel on 4-inch blocks and tie it to the posts. This 4-inch gap allows for weed control but is not so large that skunks can burrow

• Once panel has been secured, use a drill to make a ¼ inch hole through the post about 12 inches down from the panel top at a horizontal bar location. Use cobalt bits to drill through rod

• Put 1/4 inch bolt from the inside to the outside through hole, using 1 washer next and then a nut and tighten

• Now screw on the second nut and washer with Loc Tite leaving 3/8 inch between the two nuts

• If done correctly, the 52-inch cattle panel rests on the bolt—all the weight rests on the bolt

INDEX

AUTHOR'S PUBLICATIONS:

Horn, Tammy. *Beeconomy: What Women and Bees Can Teach Us about Local Trade and the Global Market*. Lexington: University Press of KY, 2012.

Horn, Tammy. *Bees in America: How the Honey Bee Shaped a Nation*. Lexington: University Press of KY, 2005.

Horn, Tammy. *"The Graphic Novel as a Choice of Weapons," Teaching the Graphic Novel*. Ed. Stephen Tabachnick. New York: Modern Language Association of America, 2003. 91-98.

Horn, Tammy. *"Honey Breeding: An Appalachian Aristaeus in Lee Smith's Fair and Tender Ladies,"* The Journal of Kentucky Studies. Highland Heights: Northern Kentucky University, 106-110.

Horn Potter, Tammy and Kunal Sharma. *"Honey Corridors in the Nilgiri Biosphere Reserve and Appalachian Coal Production Areas"* Global Mountain Regions: Conversations toward the Future. Eds. Anne Kingsolver and Sasikumar Balasundaram. Bloomington, Indiana UP, 2018. 297-314.

Horn Potter, Tammy, Patrick Angel, Carl Zipper, Michael Ulyshen, Michael French, Jim Burger, Mary Beth Adams. "Re-establishing Pollinator Habitat on Mined Lands Using the Forestry Reclamation Approach," Forest Reclamation Advisory #14, Feb. 2017. https://arri.osmre.gov/FRA/Advisories/FRA-14-ReestablishingPollinatorHabitat-Feb2017.pdf

Author's contact address:

Tammy Horn Potter, KY State Apiarist

Kentucky Department of Agriculture

109 Corporate Drive

Frankfort, KY 40601

502.229.2950

tammy.potter@ky.gov

CPSIA information can be obtained
at www.ICGtesting.com
Printed in the USA
FSHW011352111119

9 781878 075567